Cleopatra's Wedding Present

TURKEY

İskenderun
(Alexandretta)
Antioch

Azaz   Manbij   •Tall Halaf
Aleppo   Al Hasakah   •Al Qamishli

Mediterranean Sea

Lake
Assad   Ar
Raqqah   Euphrates   Zalabiyah
(Al Furat)   (Zenobia)

Qalat Salah
al Din   Idlib   •Ebla
Latakia   Al Qardahah   Al Ghab Valley   Madinat ath
Thawrah   Dayr az
Zawr
Jablah   Apamea   Isriyah

Qalat
al Madiq   Hamah   2,845 ft+
Tartus   S   Y   R   I   A

Tripoli   Hims   ◊ Palmyra
Al Qusayr   Mari
Abu Kamal

LEBANON   6,070 ft+
Beirut   Jabal ar Ruwaq   2,077 ft +

Sab Abar
Mt. Hermon
9,232 ft   Damascus   Jabal at Tanf
2,533 ft +   IRAQ
Majdal Shams   JARAMANAH
REFUGEE CAMP
Al Mansurah   Al Mazzah   3,258 ft
Tall Abu an Nada   Al Qunaytirah
3,950 ft   GOLAN
Sea of Galilee   HEIGHTS   Jabal ad Duruz
5,906 ft
ISRAEL

Busra
ash Sham   JORDAN
WEST
BANK   •Amman
Jerusalem

◊ Gas field
⌂ Oil field
— Pipeline
∴ Ruin

0   50
MILES

Cleopatra's Wedding Present

Travels Through Syria

Robert Tewdwr Moss

Duckworth

Reprinted July 1998
Paperback edition March 1998
First published in 1997 by
Gerald Duckworth & Co. Ltd.
The Old Piano Factory
48 Hoxton Square, London N1 6PB
Tel: 0171 729 5986
Fax: 0171 729 0015

A catalogue record for this book is available
from the British Library

ISBN 0 7156 2846 1

Typeset by Ray Davies
Printed in Great Britain by
Redwood Books Ltd, Trowbridge

Contents

For Afsaneh

1

Syria

The hot wind that had carried the early heat wave into town was laden with fine brown dust and clotted with diesel fumes, so that when it abated the suffocating heat laced with dirt hung like a cloak around us and grey clouds loomed above the chaos of the streets. The dangerous choreography of people and cars continued to unfold in the road, but with an added intensity. As the sky darkened, pedestrians threw themselves before the vehicles with extra zeal, while a dissonant ensemble of klaxons and horns improvised an increasingly irritable rebuke.

Many of the cars I could see were very handsome, and probably older than I was. Mercedes, Bristols and Dodges, Chevrolets, Citroëns and Peugeots surged past, all dating from the French Mandate period and conserved for a productive and gallant old age, here in this strangely cut-off northern city of Aleppo, the conservative and widely disliked rival of Damascus. I raised my hand to stop one and it drew up beside us, beautiful but battered, like a noble warhorse clanking into the lists beneath an armour of rotting chrome.

The houses we drove past were old too, cloaked in wooden weatherboarding and decorated with carved shutters that had once been beautiful. Now their intricate decorations and textures were drowned in the grime of pollution and smothered with hundreds of trashy plastic signs covered in Arabic scrawl which meant nothing to me.

From the outside, the Baron Hotel – squat, grey, built of stone – looked all those things that buildings which are the sole relicts of a distant age do look: a fortress braving the change and decay all around it, the last outpost of faded splendour in an otherwise rackety and filthy town. When I entered the stone-flagged hall, an overweight retriever bitch was peeing on the floor. She raised herself up

with difficulty from her rear haunches and staggered slowly to a
remote corner in the shadows, where she flopped down onto the
tiles, her body heat draining into the cool stone. In the men's
cloakroom it looked as though the customers had been following her
example.

Unperturbed by first impressions, I went to the desk and asked for
a room. A room for two. After all, this was once one of the premier
hotels of the eastern Mediterranean, retaining enough of its former
reputation to justify at least a drink in its expensive and unluxurious
bar. And even if the entrance hall was not exactly the gothic film set
I had been hoping for, maybe the old chaises longues, tubs of palms
and ottomans had been shunted upstairs. Lawrence of Arabia had
stayed here, as had Lady Mountbatten, Theodore Roosevelt, and the
aviators Charles Lindbergh and Amy Johnson. Would it have been
so spartan in those days?

The manager was a correctly dressed man who politely informed
me that as it was high season the hotel was full, but that if I and my
friend cared to wait in the bar for a while, he was anticipating that a
room would be coming free in about half an hour. As the Baron was
about half the price of the anodyne Ramsis Hotel opposite, but had
more (how shall I put it?) 'atmosphere' (the quality that generally
replaces style, comfort and service in such establishments), we decided to wait, even though the room – in accordance with the
government's latest requirements – had to be paid for in dollars.

The manager conducted us to the bar, empty save for a large
red-faced, distinctly overweight Englishman whom I felt I had seen
before. He was precariously balanced on a little stool with a Box
Brownie camera in front of him. Of the many odd things about him,
I could not decide whether it was his voice or his complexion which
was the most peculiar. The latter was an angry red colour, and his
shiny face was puffed up out of all proportion to his features, like a
buffalo tomato. He looked as if he might be due for the most
almighty heart attack at any minute. His voice clearly had difficulty
escaping from the series of chins and dewlaps that contained it, and
it was tarry and indistinct, as though issuing through a tiny mega-
phone. But when it did finally emerge it was with a clipped,
old-fashioned accent larded with the stock phrases his generation
tend to use to keep the conversation chugging along while the mind
lays traps.

'You come from Iran, do you?' he said, turning to my companion

Mammad. 'How fascinating. A very beautiful country, Persia.' He shifted his attention to me. 'And you a writer, you say? Well, what a surprise, so am I. What did you say your name was? Richard Tudor Moore? Yes, you're famous, aren't you. Well, I certainly know the name. Mine's Farson, by the way. Dan Farson.' I certainly knew the name, too, as we shared mutual acquaintances. 'So you're staying here too? Good. Sharing a room?' he asked casually.

Suddenly he glanced through the double doors into the dining room and downed his drink in one gulp. At the far end of the room, by the French windows, a grey-haired lady was being helped into her chair by the manager. As she sat down, he slid her chair under the table. It almost came up to her chin, giving her the look of a wizened child. It transpired that this was the Baron's owner, sole proprietress since the death of her husband Coco Maslumian two years previously. He was an Armenian and allegedly a baron.

As the final destination of those few Armenian Turks who escaped being slaughtered, dismembered, slowly frozen or starved to death on the long enforced march across Turkey before the Ottoman army in 1915, Aleppo today boasts a thriving Armenian business population. Many Armenians work with gold, which is by Koranic tradition forbidden to Moslems. It struck me as ironic that while in our civilization it is the Jews who are associated with money-grubbing and diamond-hocking, in the Arab world it is the Christians.

'Look, please forgive me, I've got to go now and interview Madame for a piece I'm writing about the hotel,' explained Farson (henceforth known to us simply as F), who went on to inform us that he was leaving early the following morning in order to attend the opening night of a production of *The Taming of the Shrew* in Damascus. 'Why don't we meet here tonight for drinks?' he suggested genially. He went on to say that he was looking forward to introducing us to the most wonderful young man, a Dane, and a poet. 'We have been having the most precious and enriching Platonic relationship since the moment we met,' he volunteered. 'Shall we say six-thirty? Splendid.' He snatched up the Box Brownie and wobbled off.

The manager returned to inform us that a room had indeed come free and, having followed a strong, lumbering young man up a couple of flights of stairs with our bags, we accepted it without further ado. Mammad and I then decided to visit the famous souks of Aleppo – not that a couple of hours could possibly do them justice, as there are over seventy-seven kilometres of covered markets specializing in different forms of merchandise: the Al Itakiyyeh (leather), the Al Hibal (rope), the Al Attarin (perfume), the As-Sakatiyyeh and the Al Bahramiyyeh (food), the Al Istanbul (gold and jewellery), and the Az-Zarb (veils, turbans and head-dresses) to name but a few. These markets run between the Great Mosque (the Jami'a Zakariyyeh, so called because it houses the head of Zacharias, father of John the Baptist) and the famous citadel of Aleppo, built, sacked and rebuilt countless times by successive waves of Persian, Mongol and Arab invaders. The Byzantine Greeks overwhelmed the town twice and the Crusaders also lay siege to it, although neither managed to take the spectacular citadel, which to this day remains Aleppo's crowning glory.

It was a Thursday evening and, having forgotten that Friday was a public holiday, neither Mammad nor I had changed any money into Syrian pounds. The banks were therefore closed until Saturday, so Mammad decided that he would change some dollars in the market. As we were in a police state where an estimated forty per cent of the population are in the employ of the government in some way, I was not particularly keen on this idea, but I reasoned that if Mammad could brave the black market of the Islamic Republic of Iran, where he had just been visiting his family, then Assad's Syria should not present an insuperable problem.

We soon found ourselves being ushered into various cloth-sellers' booths and proffered little glasses of tea. One young man seemed to keep a teapot permanently to hand under his counter. 'Sit, sit, take te-e-ea? take te-e-ea?' he asked, with the delightfully prolonged rising cadences the Syrians use when asking a question. Soon we were sipping a delicately perfumed and refreshing leaf tea from dainty gold-rimmed glasses. I asked him what he put in his tea to make it taste of violets. 'Misk, misk,' he hissed back like a cat and, gabbling instructions in Arabic, sent a boy running to the tea souk whence he returned carrying a small sachet of white crystals that looked like cocaine. 'Here, add to tea but not too much, you can try for yourself,' said the stallholder.

Mammad and I caught each other's eye, both of us wondering how to get on to the subject of filthy lucre. We wriggled on our stools, twizzling our tiny glasses around in order to make a show of admiring them while congratulating our host on his tea-making abilities and in particular his dextrous use of misk. Could we trust our new acquaintance not to rush off and shop us to the nearest branch of the secret police? In the end we need not have worried.

'Now here we have fine Syrian silk, only two hundred Syrian pounds,' said our host, who appropriately was called Aladdin. 'Very beautiful silk. A scarf for your wife, sir? You are married? You are not married. Very well, for your sister.' Then, in an undertone accompanied by much swirling of gaudy material: 'Change dollars? Change dollars? I give you good rate.' Cloth wafted over Mammad's lap. 'Is a deal, OK? Wait, I get you money. Yes, sir. Here, I put it in the bag and fold it up for you very nice and small. There we are, sir. And it has been a pleasure to do business with you.'

Extricating ourselves from the souk proved difficult. The corridors were tall and vaulted, interspersed with ancient khans, the sleeping quarters for the traders and their beasts who had journeyed from such towns as Mosul in Iraq (which gave the world muslin) in long-since-defunct caravanserais. Inside, it was dark and cool, the walls being made of stone with tiny round skylights let into them very high up. Not only did one covered corridor look confusingly like another, but Aladdin had put us on the trail of his friends and relatives, or rather had put them onto ours. Soon, out of sheer exhaustion, we felt it necessary to collapse at their stalls, if only to recover our breath. After about half a minute we realized that this was a mistake, as we were soon surrounded by chattering young stallholders, more eager to clap eyes on our wares than the other way round. 'Please, sir, take tea with us. Do not fear. It is nothing to worry about,' said one strange white-faced youth called Boy George, who had pale, mystical, staring blue eyes. 'It is only our Syrian bestiality. I'm sorry, hospitality.'

One of the young assistants introduced me to his good-looking friend James – an anglicization of his Arabic name, Hisham. James spoke English with a politically correct gay inflection crossed with Cockney, and declared himself to be a former employee of Heaven. From life under the arches of Aleppo to life under the arches of the Embankment – it must have been quite a shock.

James was more than happy to prattle on about it, talking about the 'pubz 'n' clubz' of Soho, Leicester Square and environs with great relish. Only weeks later, by chance, did I discover that James had never in his life set foot outside Syria, and that he had learned all his English and his intricate knowledge of the fleshpots of WC2 from men he had picked up in the souk. The Syrians have a brilliant gift for languages which is entirely rooted in business. All the young market traders had learned their English, French, German and Italian from tourists, and, since the demise of the Soviet empire and the arrival over the border of thousands of desperate Russian Olgas touting their black bin-bags full of ghastly Russian goodies, they had acquired a proficient knowledge of Russian too. The vast majority of them had never been and, in the current situation, never would go to Europe, but their appetite for learning and their inventiveness, their love of puns and wordplay, were seemingly inexhaustible and utterly exhausting, as we had by now discovered, sitting paralysed with fatigue in the umpteenth booth, quaffing the umpteenth glass of sticky tea. Time was drawing on, and by now we were late for our rendezvous at the Baron.

One boy rushed after us. He had the widest blue eyes in the world, set in a pale face with long black lashes. A moonchild. 'Excuse me, sir, where do you stay?' he implored. 'You stay at the Baron?' Got it in one. 'Very well. I come there at seven o'clock tomorrow night. Oh, you are very nice. We meet on the terrace, yes?' Yes. I smiled wildly, not wishing to get further embroiled, grateful that the affirmative gave me the chance of escape. I ran after Mammad over the now deserted cobbled alleyways. Where would I be tomorrow night? Could I afford the Baron? Should I go and see *The Taming of the Shrew* in Damascus? 'See you later,' we called, exiting through the gathering darkness.

2

A Fellow Englishman

By the time we had traced our way back to the hotel I was virtually on my knees with exhaustion. I gesticulated to Mammad that I was going to take a bath and stole across the hall, while Mammad went into the bar. As I darted past the door, I saw two faces turn towards him, one wooden, handsome, freakishly Nordic, the other puce, quivering, pop-eyed.

In the gloom at the top of the baronial staircase, I encountered a withered crone moving slowly beneath a ragged black gown, her thin skull bound in a scarf, her chin, long Semitic nose and waxen cheekbones emerging in four peaks. From the rag, a claw extended, holding another rag, with which she was slowly polishing the one article of furniture on display: an old cedarwood chest inlaid with pieces of mother of pearl and ivory. She looked like the wicked queen from *Snow White*: a djinn.

Emerging from the bath, I sifted through my battered belongings, looking for something to wear. In doing so I began to take in a few equally run-down features of the bedroom: the heavy cotton curtains flapping at the ends because half their rings were missing, the curly interlaced letters of the BH insignia on the bed linen, the extraordinarily cumbersome old central heating radiators of almost industrial dimensions, *circa* 1930, redolent of those in the house in which I grew up, cast iron with a raised seam running along the outside of each ridge.

I selected a white linen shirt frayed at the seams, a dark blue cravat with tiny white dots, and a voluminous pair of navy blue linen trousers to which I attached a suitable fascist-looking belt, then doused myself with a few splashes of Malmaison by Floris and waited a few seconds for the rich, heady shock of carnation to assail my nostrils. Home at last. Perfume is the one luxury I allow myself when travelling into the unknown. It is evocative of comfort and dinner at eight, of the past but only the fragrant past, of the promising near future, of changing gear in the transition from one situation to another, a new start. I've worn it so long it is an extension of myself. Sometimes, I reflected, traversing the empty hall, it was just a question of environment control, a sort of ectoplasm: zap your own effluvium before the bad plumbing, sewage and body odour zap you. Could be useful in Aleppo if what I had been told about the drains was correct.

Pomaded and pomandered, I descended to the bar where I found Mammad, the Dane and F apparently comfortably ensconced. I wafted up to the table. Mammad sneezed.

Apart from some drab oriental watercolours, the bar was unenlivened by any item of furniture or decoration which was not functional. The low-watt lighting wobbled unkindly overhead. The table at which we sat was a wasteland of used glasses, empty beer cans and overflowing ashtrays. Lying among the detritus was one of F's books, gushingly inscribed with a few sentences to his new friend, glowing with optimism and hope with regard to their new association. The author was in full flow.

'Oh, dear me, no, a trip to Petra is not the great adventure it once was. They'll all be there now. Busloads of them being led round by the nose in parties.'

Eventually introductions were effected with the Dane, who was called Nils. F went into panegyrics about the beauty, the intensity, the absolute rightness of his new 'relationship', as he insisted on calling it. He knew someone in London who edited a poetry magazine, and he fully intended asking him – no, indeed, telling him – to publish some of the Dane's immortal lines of poesy. Nils went to get some cigarettes. 'Of course, our relationship is purely Platonic, and that's what is so very beautiful about it,' confided F when he had left.

The book on the table was a guide to Turkey. It was, it announced on the cover, 'fully updated'. What it didn't include were details of how much it cost for the services of a willing youth, a subject upon which, having moved on from Platonism, F was now expatiating.

'I managed to get one back to the hotel. I tell you, it was the first time for me in sixteen years. Yes, you might well look surprised. You might well say "Oh, golly". So I had it out with him as we went past the reception desk. "The price you are asking for *that carpet* is absurd," I said. "For that sort of money it would have to be a *bloody good carpet*. Well, you'd better come up to my room so we can come to a final decision about the amount I am going to pay you for *this carpet*".'

'You should take a stroll in the souk,' suggested Mammad after F had concluded his anecdote.

'Mammad was a great success, to his surprise,' I added indiscreetly. 'There was quite a retinue following him in the market. One of them wants to come here for a drink tomorrow night.'

F's goggling eyes, very white against his trembling red-veined physiognomy, swung round like cannons fastening upon their target. 'You were picking up young men in the souk?' he spluttered incredulously. 'You don't waste any time, by Jove, do you, young man?' His jowls quivered in outrage, like those of a headmaster in an Ealing comedy, although he was clearly titillated as well. 'And how many of these "boys", as you put it, were there?'

'Did I say that? Anyway, it's not important. About seven or ten, I imagine.'

'Not important? You invite boys to this hotel and you don't even know how many? So when are they coming? Having them up in your room, I suppose. One by one. One by bloody one. Isn't that right?'

'I think we'd better go to dinner,' murmured Mammad judiciously, hoping to pre-empt F's mind overheating with his vision of our imagined debauchery.

'Wait a minute,' said F, suddenly becoming imploring, aware that he might be left alone. 'Just another drink before we all go?'

Breathing heavily, he heaved himself into a standing position, rocking the table so that several glasses teetered dangerously on the edge. He took a few uncertain steps towards the bar, like a toddler in nappies, one arm raised, trying to catch the eye of the barman. 'Another round of the same for my friends,' he announced to the room at large. A lost-looking Japanese couple, clad in Aquascutum, looked up at him from across the bar. Heads turned in the dining room. Suddenly he spun round, pointing a quavering, denouncing finger at me. 'But nothing, nothing for this character,' he shouted. 'I wish it to be known that ... that ... that person is nothing whatever to do with me.'

* * *

The Al Kebob is a lively restaurant down a little side alley opposite the Baron. Through a porch, we entered a large courtyard overshadowed by an old eucalyptus tree. Each of the little square tables scattered around the yard was taken. The waiter obligingly fixed one up for us just next to the tree trunk, and we sat down to contemplate a menu, chalked up on a blackboard in Arabic on one side and English on the other. Mammad ordered chicken kebab. I ordered something mysteriously called 'birds'.

Although the restaurant was full to capacity, there was not one woman to be seen. All the waiters – and presumably the chefs too – were men. Women in Syria are rarely employed on domestic duties on the grounds that they could be a temptation to the male employees, who would therefore not perform their tasks satisfactorily. What this actually means is that few hotels – apart from five-star ones – are as clean as they could be, nor are meals in restaurants as appetizing or inventive or varied as one would hope. Indeed, the food in Syria can be gallingly routine: houmous swimming in olive oil, kebabs, roast chicken, plate upon plate of fart-inducing beans. Chickpeas are the mainstay of every collation – stewed, boiled or even raw. You can eat falafels until they come out of your ears.

Deformed and malnourished cats flitted among the tables, where groups of men sat talking, some dressed in the traditional djellabah, some in dull grey business suits and ties. The tie, not popular in Iraq or Iran (where it is banned for being too decadent), is an acceptable form of neckwear in this part of the world, favoured by both President Assad and King Hussein of Jordan, two very different leaders. The latter is shown wearing one with a suit on his country's banknotes, accessorizing it rather innovatively with the red-and-white head-dress so symbolic of Arab identity, thus fusing Western leanings with Arab tradition. Assad, on the other hand, echoes the style of the Soviet apparatchik, and in particular the now extinct general secretaries of the Soviet Communist Party who formerly lurked behind his regime. His is therefore an anti-Western statement. As the Soviets were against God and for the equality of the sexes, the majority of organized objectors to Assad's regime have clustered around the pole representing values diametrically opposed to Soviet ones: that of the Islamic fundamentalist Moslem Brotherhood, pro-God, pro-veil, anti the equality of the sexes. Anti-tie. Thirty thousand of the latter had been exterminated overnight only twelve years previously. Aleppo is one of the main areas of dissent against the government, even though it is close to Lattakia and the area where the President's family comes from.

The most fashionably dressed women in Syria are probably those connected to the President's sect, the Alouites. In Aleppo, they dine in the more expensive eateries in the chic Christian quarter where the upmarket boutiques and brasseries are to be found. Here, beautiful, stylish women with long black hair, platform shoes, flared trousers, pale faces and brilliant blue eyes – the typical Syrian colouring – can occasionally be glimpsed. Looking at them, it is hard to tell if they are Christian or members of the Alouite ruling class. In any case, both are minority groups, and each has a healthy regard for the other. The regime understands what it is like to be part of a minority.

Such was the nature of the discussion Mammad and I had while waiting for the 'birds' to arrive. The dish in question turned out to be a large plate heaped with the carcasses of sparrows. I inspected the minuscule cadavers to see if the entrails had been deep-fried along with the rest of the body. I decided they probably had. The birds tasted quite rich and livery, with the gamey flavour of offal. Thankfully the heads and bills had been removed. We also had a very basic salad – sprays of spring onions, big leaves of lettuce, whole radishes and tomatoes. The chicken kebab was as you might expect. Our assessment of our new diet was unfortunately terminated by a looming presence hovering over the table and the appearance of a pudgy hand by the pepper mill steadying a tottering, overweight frame. It was F.

'I simply can't believe your nerve. First you destroy what was most precious and pure for me. Then you brazenly come here. Here, to my favourite restaurant, and usurp *my* table.' He was banging his fist on the tablecloth so that the little birds hopped up and down on their plate. 'Well, you might be interested to know that I've had a word with Madame at the hotel and informed her of your little plan for tomorrow night and she was less than impressed. I don't think you're going to find it at all easy to stay at the Baron again.' He smacked his lips triumphantly. 'And what is more I've cancelled my trip to *The Taming of the Shrew* so I can see exactly what is going on. I shall inform the Chief of Police and put an end to your antics. And by Jove, sonny, if I see you again, I shall make it my job to destroy you and your career.' In between threats he was snatching up the bodies

of the birds and stuffing them into his mouth – naked little ornitho-
logical corpses, sliding down into the maws of hell.

He twisted round, his eyes boggling in Mammad's direction. 'As
for you,' he snarled, a sparrow leaping from his mouth, 'you're no
more Persian than I am. You're a complete fraud. All you're interested in is picking up English boys and fucking them in hotel rooms.
Don't think I don't know your little game.'

I could see Mammad's brow darkening, and his brown eyes
flashed dangerously. He had grown up in Qom, one of Iran's most
puritanical cities, under the shadow of the Ayatollah Khomeini,
whom he had known personally until he left to go to Tehran
University at the age of eighteen. He hadn't, thank God, taken after
the Ayatollah, although he was still very spiritual.

I noticed the Danish poet sitting rigidly at a table at the back of
the courtyard. 'You'd better be getting off to your dinner,' I cau-
tioned F. 'Can't you see you're insulting him? The guy's straight.'

Two waiters appeared, followed by the poet, crimson to the roots
of his platinum hairline. 'I am sorry, sir,' one waiter said politely,
taking F by the elbow.

'He's taken my table,' I heard F whimper like a little boy as they
led him, almost in tears, towards the door.

'I am very sorry, sir,' the waiter repeated over his shoulder.

Such beautiful manners, the Arabs.

I spent a fretful night. There was an open-air restaurant on the roof
of the building next to the Baron and I kept waking to hear Arabic
pop music, animated conversation and the rattle of dishes. In the
dark, I could see a huge triangle at the window, like the sail of a
yacht, where the curtain, unsupported by hooks, had drooped down.
I woke again a few hours later to silence, apart from the squalling of
an alley cat. Dawn was breaking, and as things gradually came into
focus I realized that the noise was not the spitting of a feral animal
but the hoarse larynx of a human being hissing a chain of exple-
tives.

'Mammad,' I whispered. 'Wake up. It's F. Outside the door.'

Mammad turned over, oblivious to my attempts to wake him. I
got up and crept over to the window, pulling back the curtain. After
a few seconds I saw F trundling across the terrace with a little
suitcase. He put it down on the pavement. He must have decided to
go to Damascus after all. Every time a taxi approached, his arm

flailed in an uncoordinated movement that looked more like an offensive gesture than a bid for attention. He was swaying slightly. Nobody stopped for him, and as each car sailed by he screamed something indistinguishable after it.

Eventually the manager appeared at his shoulder. A minibus approached. The manager hailed it and it slowed to a halt. The door slid open and the manager placed the little suitcase inside. F managed to get one foot onto the step and heaved his dead weight upwards, holding onto a seat. For one awful moment he swayed backwards and forwards and backwards again until the manager clamped a hand on his rear. And pushed.

At breakfast the next morning there was a selection of faded old European ladies in the dining room, looking like characters from a Barbara Pym novel. They were nibbling at sliced bread and bits of cheese. Most of them, like myself, ignored the olives that accompanied them in a little bowl. The thought of olives for breakfast – also a Turkish custom – was something that I (raised, I am ashamed to say, on a convenience breakfast of Weetabix and bucketfuls of sugar to shock the system into action) could barely contemplate. Mammad, however, happily popped one after another into his mouth, spitting the stones out onto his plate. 'I never say no to olives,' he remarked, as though they were champagne or hand-made Belgian chocolates.

That day we had agreed to go with a driver from the Baron to Ain Dera, the ruined acropolis in the middle of nowhere which was once home to a Hittite temple dedicated to the evocatively named goddess Ishtar. It was built in 1000 BC and destroyed two centuries later. Since the fifties archaeologists have been uncovering strange cartoon-like black basalt reliefs of lions and sphinxes, suns, moons and elephants. The most extraordinary is of a vast lion lying on its side with its tongue hanging out. One day the lion is going to be rehoused in its rightful place, which, according to Syrian heritage, would appear to be in the middle of a series of concrete pillars in the process of being erected on the acropolis in an attempt to recreate the old temple. On the way to Ain Dera we planned to stop at the famous ruins of Qala'at Samaan, the Byzantine church of St Simon Stylites, a Syrian shepherd who sat atop a fifteen-metre pillar for thirty years, with a chain around his neck attached to a railing so that he would not fall to his death. The pillar remains to this day – eroded and whittled away by pilgrims – in the form of a rather amorphous boulder.

The manager – who had a habit of appearing discreetly – appeared discreetly at my elbow to inform us that the our car would soon be ready. He then cleared his throat. 'I must say, sir, with respect. Your friend, Mr F.'

'Yes?' I said, dreading what might follow.

'Extraordinary. Quite extraordinary. I have been here for over thirty-five years and in all that time, sir, I have never, ever come across a man who could drink so much alcohol. He started two hours before you arrived at the hotel and last night his friend left him on the terrace, with a bottle of I think gin or maybe vodka. He was there until five o'clock this morning on his own. Drinking. Drinking and, you know, er, speaking with himself.'

Suddenly I felt depressed. I had visions of F, slumped on a chair in the dark, with a bottle and no glass. Just slowly downing it and raging against the dying of the night, the coming of the day, snarling into the illimitable pit of the universe.

'He spent a lot of money in our bar here, sir,' added the manager, his eyes gleaming. 'A very great deal indeed. He bought many drinks. Many drinks for many people.'

Poor old F. Something could be said of him, at least: inebriated, sober or sodden to the core, he had that outward generosity that is always an attractive quality. Perhaps to be truly generous-hearted you have to love your fellow man, be concerned about his comfort and happiness. And for people like that life can have a habit of going terribly wrong.

3

Cupid's Bow

After Mammad left Aleppo I decided for reasons of economy to leave the Baron. I settled on the Rose of Aleppo, tucked away in the downmarket Bab El Faraj area of the city. I was guided to it by a swift-witted young merchant called Adnan whom Mammad and I had met in the souk.

From street level the hotel was totally concealed from view save for a small green-and-white electric sign. To get to reception you had to go upstairs past clothes wholesalers whose rows and rows of ugly 'Western' garments were hung with signs in Russian for the benefit of the new wave of Russian hawkers who had recently descended on the city. A staircase into the basement led to a printer's, whose huge presses, when in action, made the whole building shudder, and from whence emanated at times a heavy inky smell.

To the right of the hotel entrance there was a tiny workshop where an old white-haired man with a square broad skull and heavy jowls worked making fezzes. He was the last fez maker in Aleppo, and had inherited the business from his father.

On our serpentine route to the hotel, Adnan alternately revolted and entertained me with candid stories of his experiences with the new crop of Russian prostitutes who had arrived in the city with the traders. I learned that the price of a Russian tart was ten dollars a go, roughly half the average national wage, which Adnan said was about fifteen to twenty dollars a week. I had no desire to use this information, but I was in a new country where even the most banal facts – the price of a bus ticket, the going rate for a room or a taxi ride – suddenly became an illuminating insight into one's environment.

At the Rose I found the rooms clean enough to permit a few days' stay. I was shown to mine by a tall slim youth with a long bony face and black hair, as floppy and shiny as a cat's. His high cheekbones, slanting eyes and wonderful patrician nose made him look like a young brave. His name was Nazmi, and he was painfully shy, but his great asset was that he played the bazuk, a form of Kurdish lute, which occasionally of an evening – when I had come to befriend him a little – he would come and play to me in bed, attended by a retinue of hotel residents with whom I developed the sort of relationship that one might with the residents of a guest house in Hove. There was a polite but tragic Palestinian alcoholic, bloated and bleary-eyed, who had worked in West Africa, a dear old man who always wore a long grey robe and flicked his burgundy worry beads back and forth, looking out of his watery blue eyes into space, and a group of Kurdish students.

I also struck up a great rapport with the proprietor's son, Abdulkabir, who seemed to me to epitomize everything that is good about the Arab character. He was hospitable, kind, polite, good-humoured, generous, caring, gallant, respectful both of his elders and his inferiors, dutiful to Islam yet accepting of all faiths. To look at he was pure Arab, with soft brown eyes of the sweetest expression, a thick, neatly trimmed black beard, and dark olive skin. Whenever I came back to the hotel in the evening he would prepare tea for us, for tea-drinking was one of his great delights.

His father owned the hotel in partnership with a formidable businesswoman in her fifties who had blond permed hair, painted nails, wore trousers and smoked continuously. She had, I felt, a slightly sinister presence, possibly due to the fact (as I later learned) that she was a 'fixer' (one of only two such women in the whole city) who had influence in the ministries. One of her skills was the bribing of officials in order to secure the release from prison of young army defectors. For this she would demand of the family concerned a sum of about ten thousand dollars, though she never issued guarantees. She was married to a distinguished elderly man whose only function in life seemed to be to sit in reception playing backgammon with Abdulkabir's father.

Having checked in, I left the hotel and strolled around the town, looking for a telephone box from which to phone Oris, a half-Armenian, half-Arab photographer whose name had been given to me by someone in England. Eventually I made my call and got through to a sensitive-sounding young man with a rather camp voice who spoke a very idiosyncratic form of English. 'Today I am on appointments. I have four appointments until three o'clock. All day

I am walking, all over Aleppo. I come your hotel at five for appointment?' Until five I was free to wander.

Passing through the Great Mosque with its huge free-standing minaret, I plunged into the souk in order to get to the citadel. The mosque was bustling, full of people of all ages – some praying, some chanting, some just slumbering in the shade of the portico or against one of the large pillars in the triple-arched prayer hall which takes its inspiration from a Byzantine church. Inside, there was none of the padlocked, mean-spirited, mildewed sanctity of the Church of England.

As I left the mosque by the back door and progressed up the slope that I imagined would lead to the citadel, I almost collided with the blue-eyed moonchild. He looked at me fruitily, with eyes growing rounder by the second. 'Squeeze me, squeeze me,' he begged saucily, rendering me for a moment nonplussed, until I realized that this was his version of 'Excuse me'. 'I am so sorry, I did not see you,' he continued. From the ironic gleam in his eye I understood that he was joking. He then affected to look hurt and pouted his cherry-red lips. 'Where were you? I came to your hotel. I waited one hour on the terrace. I wrote a letter to you. Why were you not there?'

I made up a lame excuse about being delayed over dinner, remembering that I had indeed received a wounded little note.

'Please stay, sit, come here,' said the moonchild – whose name was Mejid – pulling me towards a fabric stall.

I professed that I was in a great hurry to visit the citadel.

'I will take you, *habibi*. Have no fear. I will show you everything,' said Mejid, undaunted by my off-handedness.

We climbed the rising cobbled slope towards a remote arch of white light. On the way Mejid waved to an older man – a more ravaged, crumpled version of himself. It was, he explained, one of his many brothers (I never did work out quite how many he had, but however many there were it made a quick trot through the souk a virtual impossibility). 'You see Ahmed, he very boring man. He straight, married with children. He not know the meaning of Willy Woofter and Gender Bender,' explained Mejid. I expressed my sorrow at this great lack in Ahmed's life.

Turning right at the archway, we emerged on the road that skirted round the great citadel. From below, the fortress's walls appeared so flat and vertical as to be two-dimensional, looking as though they might fall flat on their faces at the merest gust of wind, like a house of cards or a film set. We followed the road round to the daunting entrance gate which reared up at the end of a great stone arched bridge leading to the castle from a chunky, muscular entrance tower. Opposite this tower were a few shops and a couple of cafés under some eucalyptus trees. Mejid spotted his friend James, the cunning linguist from the souk, sitting at a table with an Englishman and a very pretty young boy.

The Englishman struck me as being somewhat unusual, in that he was neither a New Age backpacker nor a middle-aged culture vulture. I thought he was probably one of those fey young men who treat Syria – this horrendous hard-line police state – as one big art gallery, swanning around from one architectural site to the next with an exotic companion in tow. At Mejid's suggestion, we joined them for tea.

The Englishman was called Rupert, and was in the Levant partly travelling and partly 'studying the lute'. He had dark brown hair, long and floppy in the fringe but short at the back, a long bony face with high cheekbones, and rather voluptuous lips in the shape of a Cupid's bow. He was wearing a voluminous white shirt with heavy, ornate gold cufflinks studded with moonstones, and a dark purple waistcoat with a paisley motif. There was a navy blue coat with gold buttons slung across the back of his chair – in Syria late winter and early spring can produce sudden changes in temperature. His accent was distinctly mannered, reedy in pitch, and his vowels were painfully squeezed, so that when he said, after ordering the tea, 'Oh, and two cakes,' I was surprised when what actually appeared with the tea were two glasses of Coke, one for James and one for the young boy.

The latter was, he explained over the introductions, called Karim and was his '*garde de corps*'. This was ludicrous, as the boy was as short as the Englishman was tall. In terms of age, I later learned that the latter was roughly double the age of the former, Karim being sixteen. He did not look as if he could protect anyone from anything, although he apparently had a black belt in judo and cast-iron stomach muscles.

Karim smiled politely and soon wandered off to sit on the wall by the citadel and play a little bamboo pipe. He was wearing a square black cap embroidered with the white crescent moons of Islam, beneath which a dark shaggy fringe of hair fell like a Shetland pony's over one finely drawn oriental eye. It turned out that Rupert had bought the cap for him in the souk. I wondered whether Karim was his little project, a doll to dress up, a way of indulging his sense of aesthetics. The relationship seemed curious. For one thing, Karim could barely speak English, and Rupert was forced to talk to him in a mixture of basic English and some colloquial Arabic that he had picked up on his travels.

After tea we all went to the citadel. It seemed to have been built, razed and rebuilt several times by Persian and Mongol invaders and Arab dynasties, although the Crusaders never managed to take it. Occasionally we came across square black holes in the walls which led to great shafts disappearing deep into the bowels of the mound on which the citadel was constructed. 'Put your hand in there,' said Mejid. 'Can you feel the air? Is it wet?' I obeyed, and found that it was. 'This is *kondishon*,' giggled Mejid, using the Arabicized word for air-conditioning. But it was not a joke. Arab castles frequently employed this system of shafts to take up air from the cool wells below and draw it up into the chambers above.

We trooped around the two mosques and the old baths, their sleepy domes blistered with round bubbly windows designed to let in coloured rings of light. Rupert rolled his eyes at a replica Roman theatre with concrete seats where contemporary concerts were now performed. He said he knew some people who were going to put on an opera there the following year. I asked what it would be and was surprised when he replied, '*Dido and Aeneas*, Purcell.' First *The Taming of the Shrew*, now *Dido and Aeneas* – not at all what I had expected of a hard-line Arab state.

We left the citadel as dusk was falling. Rupert was going to the hammam with Karim, but he gave me his hotel number and said that we must meet up with his friends from the opera. I realized that time was passing, and that I needed to hurry back to the Rose to meet Oris, the photographer. Mejid said the best way to Bab El Faraj was by collective taxi, or 'servees', as it is known. This was a delightful proposition, as I had longed to try one of these ever since arriving in Aleppo. Most of them were old Chevrolets or Oldsmobiles, many of them painted with domestic paint the colour of egg yolk. They held about eight people including the driver. On the dashboard was a wooden till with coins in some sections and chewed-up notes in others. The latter were so old that they were furry and brown, often disintegrating, but they were never refused. They would be gingerly placed into wallets and purses and then Sellotaped and reused until all pecuniary life had been drained from them.

We alighted at the old clock tower. Rather to my irritation, Mejid

followed me. As we reached the door of the hotel I turned to him.
'Well, Mejid, it's been lovely. I must go now. You see, I have an
appointment.'

He looked disappointed. 'When can I see you again, *habibi*?' he
asked.

'Twelve o'clock,' I replied.

'Twelve o'clock tonight?' he asked cheekily.

'No, twelve tomorrow in the souk,' I said, feeling like a hypocrite.
I had no intention of turning up.

I climbed wearily up the stairs of the hotel, registering the tremors
caused by the printing press below. In reception the manager, Kamal,
was sitting walrus-like in front of the television, which was broadcasting a Turkish channel – a young male pop singer with long black
hair, tight jeans and cowboy boots, sinewy girls with bared midriffs
gyrating around him. Twenty miles up the road. Another planet.
Kamal was unfailingly polite but his questions about where I had
been that day and what I was going to do the next made me uneasy.

'Your frien' Oris telephone. He say he cannot come now. You
meet him in the bar at the Baron Hotel at eight tomorrow night.' I
thanked him for the message and went to my room.

I got out one of the postcards I had bought from the café near the
citadel and sat looking at the small white square of card in front of
me. How to describe Aleppo, this strange, dirty, collapsing town? A
rusty casket studded with priceless gothic gems? An ornate chalice
slowly dissolving in a bath of corrosive acid? A rich cake heaving
inside with maggots? Aleppo is finished now, I thought. Its halcyon
days as one of the premier cities of Islam, its privileges and status
enshrined in special treaties with Venice, had come to an end eight
hundred years ago. Gone was the boom of the fifteenth century,
when the fantastic khans, replete with banks, inns, stables and
everything a visiting merchant might require, were established for
the caravans and the resident European traders. Now the best the
Silk Route could provide was enamel bowls from Peking.

I looked out of the window at the citadel, which now looked like
an ancient sandcastle, then turned back to the card and wrote:
'Aleppo is a town with a great past and no present. A town that has
suffered a decline of spectacular and almost tragic proportions. It
reminds me of the old merchants you see here – sly, leathery, a
survivor – caught slightly unawares, turning its attention for the first
time to its past – to see how much it will fetch.'

4

Sunset in Serjilla

When I arrived at the Baron the next evening the bar was full of middle-aged Germanic tourists, mainly women with rinses. I sat on a stool and ordered an expensive gin and tonic. Above the barman's shoulder there was a long-out-of-date whisky advert. It read: 'White Horse: as distinctive as a traditional English club'.

The woman perched on the stool next to me would not have been allowed anywhere near a traditional English gentleman's club. She looked like all the other women in her party: permed dyed-blond hair, about fifty or sixty years old. Recognizing my accent, she broke off her conversation with her German cronies and asked me in a pronounced Mid West drawl whether it was true that the Queen had discovered oil in Windsor Great Park and was going to keep all the proceeds. I was not able to furnish her with an answer, but could not resist asking her how she had derived her authentic American accent. 'From a GI,' she said, sounding just like one, 'after the war. I worked in base camp for six years. It was just great. We got everything we wanted. Food, nylons, toilet paper ...'

At this point we were interrupted by an impish man whose bald head had the distinctive flat back of the Caucasian. He had ironic, droopy brown eyes which shimmered behind round glasses. He was wearing a colourful chunky jumper and looked as though he might be Italian. 'Are you Robert?' he asked.

'Oris?' I said as we shook hands.

He smiled. 'I never thought it would be so difficult to find one Englishman in Aleppo. In our history there were many Europeans here. The khans were full of European traders. Now no one. Only in Icarda. We go from here now? I take you back to my house.'

We left the Baron and its slew of Teutonic tourists for the cold streets.

'I live Azizieh. You know Azizieh?'

I said I did not, so Oris took me on a detour, talking volubly, ingeniously pushing the few grammatical structures he knew to encompass a range of meanings. He seemed like a tuning fork, sensitive to everything surrounding him. Azizieh, he said, was once the most exclusive area of Aleppo, built around the time of the Great War in the closing years of the Ottoman Empire. His parents' flat was in a street called Baby Shoes, he explained, after the Aleppan habit of describing a road by the merchandise that characterized it. 'If you take taxi and you tell him Baby Shoes, he take you my house no problem.'

We arrived at a street corner where there was a shop window with a lining of thick yellow cellophane glued snugly against it, behind which, in an amber pool, swam countless examples of tiny baby booties. They looked almost edible. Above it in Arabic I could just make out a sign: 'Shoes Bebe'. Further along the street we passed similar windows before turning abruptly into a shadowy doorway and starting up several flights of steep stairs. The hallway was gloomy and there was no lift.

Oris's Armenian mother opened the door. She was small, stout, with a kind oval face and a blunt nose surrounded by frizzy hair. Looking at her, I wondered how on earth she managed to scale Everest every day with her shopping. The drawing room into which she led us was notable principally for a vast paraffin stove plonked in the middle – round, shiny and black, with silver claw feet pointing in opposite directions. On the top, in an attempt to soften this uncompromising shape, was a frilly crocheted mat. This and the odd bar fire elsewhere in the flat was the only form of heating. Occasionally, way below in the street, I could hear the paraffin sellers passing by, their carts weighed down by large, garishly painted barrels and drawn slowly by depressed-looking, blinkered ponies. They would punctuate their cries with the sharp tap-tap of a spanner on a barrel.

Dinner would have been a harmonious affair had it not been for a phantom phone caller disrupting the conversation. The telephone rang repeatedly and the anonymous caller would play classical music for a few minutes before putting the phone down. Oris said this was quite a well-known trick in Aleppo. On the second occasion he asked the silent caller whether they could play any Mozart. Several minutes later we were interrupted again by the telephone ringing and strains of Mozart came through the earpiece. Oris giggled excitedly and asked for some jazz. Accordingly jazz was produced several minutes later. He then handed the telephone to me and I spoke into it in English. The phantom caller mimicked my accent. 'We're rather bored with your selection,' I said. 'Could you play us some Gregorian chant?'

'Of course I can't play Gregorian chant, dummy,' replied the voice (female) bad-temperedly. Suddenly the line went dead. Oris's father had ripped the telephone out of the socket, presumably as an assertion of his authority. Oris looked at his father, who was standing glowering, holding the deracinated telephone line in his hand. Oris's brother Victor looked at me and said, 'Now there's going to be a row.'

Oris and his father started exchanging heated words in Arabic. His mother looked embarrassed and tried to treat it all as a joke, but her hands fluttering on the arm of her chair betrayed her distress. Eventually she started remonstrating with Oris in Armenian, getting sucked in the way one does in family rows. The father, feeling excluded as he could not speak Armenian, shouted back at her in Arabic.

Oris strode to the door. 'Come, Robert, we go from here now,' he said petulantly. 'I don't want to live with them any more. I'm going. *And*,' he announced vengefully to me, but looking at them, 'I take my *carpet* with me.' He swept off to his bedroom and emerged with a carpet rolled under one arm. 'Now I go live with my uncle,' he declared. 'Come, we go now.'

I stood up, feeling horribly implicated. Oris's parents followed us from the drawing room, smiling effusively, and shook my hand. Oris ran out of the flat. I followed him guiltily, also smiling and shrugging my shoulders. The parents smiled back and shrugged their shoulders too. As we descended the cold dark spirals of the staircase, a torrent of abuse in Arabic followed by another in Armenian pursued us. Then the door slammed definitively.

As we plunged into the night, I asked where we were going. Oris replied that he was going to a reception at the Amir Palace Hotel to launch a jazz festival in which he was involved. He was organizing a competition for young people to photograph the artists. The darkroom would be in his uncle's flat near Tellal – the Oxford Street of Aleppo – where we first had to deposit the carpet. Fortunately his uncle did not live there, having removed himself to Kassab, the Armenian mountain village in northern Syria near the Turkish border.

By the time we arrived at the Amir Palace, Oris had calmed down. The reception, on the top floor of the hotel, was a dreary affair. For some reason no alcohol was served, and waiters drifted around with sickly fruit cocktails and glasses of Coke. The atmosphere was like that of any European launch party, besuited men trailing round with their trophy wives, eyes flitting around busily to see if there was anybody more interesting to talk to. It reminded me of so many aspects of my past life in London, from which I was longing to escape, that I was finding it quite depressing. The Arabs are so much better when they behave as Arabs, when their hospitality is beyond compare. The pastiche European cocktail party was a mistake. The most interesting thing in the room was the view out of it, the floodlit citadel rearing like a great bleached boat out of the mundane grey concrete sea surrounding it.

A voice drew me away from the window. 'Ah, m'dear, you *are* here. I thought I might find you.' It was Rupert, looking Byronic in a floppy white shirt and an equally floppy polka-dot bow tie. Floppiness somehow suited him. He was without Karim, who was apparently meeting him – tactfully, I thought – outside later.

'But let me introduce you to my friend Oris,' I said, as the latter hopped gremlin-like into view. 'Oris is a photographer and lives in a street called Baby Shoes.'

'How absolutely perfect,' wittered Rupert excitedly, taking in Oris with one swift, appraising glance, adding, 'I cannot imagine a sweeter name for a street, nor indeed for you. I hope you don't mind, but from now on I will always think of you as Baby Shoes.' And so Baby Shoes he became.

The 'opera crowd', as Rupert called them, was also present. The director, a young woman called Caroline Sharman, explained that she had been whisked around the country in a ministry car to research venues for the production. She had already chosen Palmyra and Bosra. I thought that to select two of the finest classical theatres in the Arab world in which to stage the famous classical love story of Dido and Aeneas was a ravishing idea. I asked her how she found the Syrian authorities, and she replied that she had been particularly surprised that they had chosen her from a shortlist of three directors, the other two being men. It was, she felt, all to Syria's credit that the first opera they had ever produced should be about a woman and be directed by a woman.

At this point the conversation came to an abrupt end. 'I'm terribly sorry,' muttered Caroline, 'I think it must be something I ate. I'm afraid you'll have to excuse me.' Before dashing off she extended an invitation to me to attend the rehearsals that were taking place during the course of the next month in Damascus.

As we were leaving, Baby Shoes suggested that the following night we should all visit his friend George (another half-Arab, half-Armenian), who lived in Suleymania, a middle-class Christian district beyond Azizieh. A figure stepped out of the shadows as we emerged from the hotel. It was Karim, looking very dashing in Rupert's paisley silk waistcoat.

Rupert, Karim and I set off in the direction of our respective hotels, which, it turned out, were very near each other. Rupert said that he had found his hotel through Karim, who knew the owners. According to him it was very cheap and much more interesting than staying in one of the homogenized five-star European hotels. 'Would you care for a drink with us?' he asked. 'I have some whisky cacao and also a bottle of Syrian champagne. It would be a good excuse to open it. I can't drink it all myself and he' – he jerked his eyes at Karim – 'gets totally sozzled after a glass. He's not allowed to drink at home. His father beats him up.'

On the way we passed a holy man's tomb draped in green cloth and surrounded by cheap artificial carpets, set in a niche in the wall of the alley that led from Rupert's hotel to mine. On two successive nights I had witnessed a strange gathering of men and boys standing around a doorway at the end of this alley, some of them holding mysterious sacks. There seemed something exclusive and faintly sinister about the gathering, and I had thought that perhaps they were flogging off contraband smuggled in from Turkey. Tonight the crowd was assembled again, men crowding round boys who were holding long black sacks. Occasionally a man would nudge his way forward and open a sack, inside which pigeons could be seen cowering. If required, a boy would lift a specimen out of his sack and hold it aloft, and potential buyers would drift by, squeezing its breast and neck. More often than not it was dumped unceremoniously back in the sack. In a derelict room at the back, more men browsed through stacks of small, rickety cages full of pigeons. All the birds were decorated with ornate leg rings and even necklaces.

One of the vendors came up to us and opened a leathery palm. In it was a pile of gaudy ornaments that appeared Indian in design – little chandeliers of enamelled tin in different colours attached to thin hoops. Clearly the Syrians decorated not only their buses, taxis, bicycles, ponies, tea vending trollies and benzine carts, but also their pigeons. The vendor put his decorations on a bench near by and took hold of a pigeon. Picking up one of the tin chandeliers, he unclasped the end and thrust it through the flesh of the bird's neck, fastening the clasp again as it emerged bloodstained on the other side. Then he thrust the poor bird, replete with bracelets and necklace, under Rupert's nose for approval. This came in the form of a watery smile. 'God, can you bear it?' he asked me out of the corner of his mouth, without aborting the smile. 'Whatever would the RSPB think of this?'

Karim pronounced the arrangement to be '*helu*' (beautiful). '*Cattir helu* (very beautiful),' added Rupert faintly.

Rupert's room was small and dark with a sloping roof and was lodged in the eaves of the old building. 'They always want Europeans to be on the same floor as reception so they can keep an eye on them,' he said. 'They say there is a mole from the Mukhabarat in every hotel. But it's always so noisy and not terribly private near reception, with the communal television set permanently on, so Karim got us this one.' Meanwhile Karim was moving about the room, lighting the petrol stove and getting glasses.

'I think I've identified the mole in the Rose already,' I said, giving Rupert a description of the sinister Kamal. I had noticed that every time I wanted to use the hotel phone, Kamal asked me to write the number down on a scrap of paper, purportedly so that he could dial for me.

'He's probably getting paid for handing them over on a piecemeal basis,' said Rupert phlegmatically. 'It might be better to phone from a local shop to protect your friends. Not, of course, that they need protecting. Or maybe they do.' He shot me a penetrating glance, but said nothing else.

The champagne was wrapped in silver foil with a curly red ribbon emerging jauntily from the top. It was made in Homs and was called Fizz Al Hayatt. 'The fizz of life,' said Rupert, translating. 'Not a bad name for champagne.' It tasted like pretty bad Lambrusco crossed with 7-Up.

'To you both,' I said.

'To you and to *al hayatt*. To life,' said Rupert.

'*Saha wa sana alla Qalbakum* (health and happiness to your

hearts),' said Karim solemnly, downing the contents of his glass as if it were a shot of vodka.

'Oops, that was a mistake, *habibi*,' said Rupert. 'It'll go straight to his head and his father will be angry with him. He has to go now. He gets locked out if he gets home after twelve at night. His father's a bit of a brute, but I'll tell you more in a minute.'

He accompanied Karim to the door. As he did so he passed him something and words were exchanged in Arabic about a taxi. Then Karim said, '*Buchra. Sa'at sebbah* (tomorrow at seven).'

Rupert came back and sat down. 'Now, more champagne or shall we make a cocktail with the whisky cacao?'

We agreed to stick with the champagne, but it was so thin and lacking in body that Rupert was soon mixing it with whisky.

'You were going to tell me about Karim,' I said. 'Where did you meet?'

He told me how he had been walking through Saad Al Jaabri square and, having no matches, had asked this young boy near the 'microbus' rank for a light. They sat on the wall together and smoked a cigarette. They began to meet every day after Karim finished work as a trainee coppersmith in the copper souk near the Joazhat. Karim had never asked him to meet his family, which was unusual for a Syrian. Rupert thought it was possible that he came from an anti-Western family, maybe one with connections in the Moslem Brotherhood who would not want to draw attention to themselves by entertaining a European. 'I don't even have his address apart from a PO box number belonging to a friend and a phone number for a sweet kiosk which his friend runs. If I leave a message there he passes it on and Karim miraculously appears at whatever time and place I specify. It's a sort of jungle telegraph system. But he's a wily little fellow. It's quite clever how he's made sure he can't be traced. Every Friday he goes to the mosque with his father and his brothers and he always wears his best clothes. Unfortunately Friday is the only day when he won't permit any, um, er, you know ...'

'Congress?' I suggested.

'Exactly.'

Rupert had returned to England but couldn't get Karim out of his head. He had returned a month ago and they had taken up where they had left off. Karim began missing work and getting into trouble, then his father had beaten him up and thrown him out of the house. He was allowed to stay in the hotel, on a different floor, and had crept into Rupert's room when everyone was asleep. That night was the first and only night they had spent together.

'He said he had never slept with anyone like me before. For the Arabs sex is quite automatic and routine. It's not really a form of protracted enjoyment. They are not awfully sophisticated as lovers, so I think being with me has been a bit of a revelation.'

'Isn't it difficult if you can't stay with him at home?' I asked.

'Of course it's difficult. I can't *tell* you about the stress. Once we were very nearly caught out. We were alone at sunset in Serjilla, one of the most beautiful of the dead cities. A goatherd suddenly squirmed out of a hole in the ground, literally. He'd been sheltering from the sun and had fallen asleep. We were lucky and managed to cover our tracks.

'But the point is you're never really alone here. There's always someone watching. Don't ever forget that. On the other hand, there is a lot of understanding, always unexpressed of course, and toler-ance, in an odd sort of way. It's a sort of compassion for the plight of the human condition. The Arabs are great fatalists. They think we have been put in a situation beyond our control and we have to make the best of it. Snatch a fearful joy and all that.'

I left soon afterwards, pondering what game was being played in the cosmos to drive two disparate individuals across continents to explore a future together. As I turned the corner of the alley leading to my hotel, the clock in Bab El Faraj was striking half past midnight. It was very cold and mist hung about the strangely deserted street. Standing on the opposite corner was a cowled figure in a long black *abbaya*, motionless, staring into the middle distance. There was about him an atmosphere of almost palpable sadness. As I turned into the darkened hall of the hotel building, I cast a glance back over my shoulder and shuddered. The figure had turned and was staring mournfully in my direction as though appealing to me. But inside the hood I could see no face, only blackness.

Crossing the River Quaik

I had noticed an old man squatting on the floor by the door of my hotel every morning selling contraband cigarettes laid out on a piece of cardboard. They were usually Pall Mall or Marlboro, some sold in packets, others singly, laid out in rows on the ground or jutting temptingly out of an open box. He was there without fail, in wind, frost, hail or sun, and as he ran out of cigarettes he made a little fire by his side with the empty cartons and any other bits of detritus that came along. The next day, on my way to meet Rupert and Karim, I noticed in the lull before the market got under way that the old vendor was not in fact squatting. He had no legs, and was balanced on his stumps on a wooden trailer with a handle with which the device could be pulled along the street. He was wedged into a coiled nest made from the extraneous folds of his grey djellabah which was tucked beneath him. Further along, in the food market by the Amir Palace, was another squatting ancient relic, a wizened, walnut-faced creature folded onto his haunches in the gutter, sorting with trembling hands through a dirty pile of grey tripe on the floor and carefully selecting pieces to place into a plastic bag. A mewing kitten hovered near by.

As agreed, I arrived at the bus station at 9 a.m. Rupert, Karim and I were going to Ebla, Maara and some of the dead cities. They were late. The cold shadow of President Hafez Al Assad fell across the square from his statue, as it falls across every town, village and home in Syria. What do the Syrians think of him? Fear? Hate? Love? The comfort of the familiar? His face is everywhere. Even in life he looks like a statue – cold, unsmiling, unmoving and unmoved.

When they eventually arrived, Rupert was effusively apologetic. They had become stuck in their room and couldn't get out. 'The door wouldn't open. It was all swollen up because of the damp. We had to knock on the wall of the room next door for someone to let us

out. It was deeply embarrassing. See what I mean about stress here?'
The excuse was so ludicrous it had the ring of authenticity.

Ebla, our first destination, proved somewhat disappointing – a
large muddy tel with geometric excavations dug out of it, dating
from different periods. Tels are the rubbish heaps of history. Syria is
full of them, mounds and mounds of history lying around, each one
consisting of dead layers of civilization superimposed one upon the
other – Sumerian, Hittite, Greek, Roman. As we scrambled up the
side of the mound the sound of pieces of Roman pottery crunching
underfoot accompanied us. With each stumbling step a little more
destruction, a little more ruin, a little more of the past gone for ever.

We reached Maaret Anuaman by flagging down a hop-hop. These
are the oldest, slowest, most uncomfortable and kitschest of Syria's
buses, often brightly painted in a naive style redolent of English canal
barges. Inside they are fussily decorated with quilted dashboards,
artificial flowers, bunting, plastic hearts holding pictures of the
President or his son (or in some cases Samantha Fox), gilt-edged
plastic Kleenex holders, and the odd evil eye or hand of Fatima to
bring good luck. On board we filled in the cards every passenger has
to complete, specifying our destination and reason for travelling.

Maara (or La Marre, as the Crusaders called it) is a town famous
for an appalling incident of cannibalism, when the Crusaders dis-
graced themselves more than usual by eating the flesh of the Saracens
during a famine. Fortunately this terrible experience has not influ-
enced the attitude of the town's present inhabitants, for after a few
minutes of aimless peregrination we were scooped up from the street
and ensconced in an office outside which loitered a large white
Jaguar. Marlboros were proffered all round. Our hosts, a group of
businessmen in suits, immediately initiated the coffee-making ritual.
None of them could speak English and it was difficult to ascertain
exactly what it was that their office sold. To help us, all manner of
swizzling devices and rotating machine parts were dangled before
our eyes, although we didn't recognize any of them. It was rather like
playing *What's My Line*. One man stood in front of us spinning his
index finger in the air like John Travolta, saying, '*Ghassaleh, ghassaleh.*' Suddenly enlightenment struck, and Rupert shouted
triumphantly, 'Washing machines! They repair washing machines!'
He later explained that he had arrived at this conclusion by virtue of
having read an Amnesty book on human rights in Syria, in which
there was a section on the forms of torture used by the Mukhabarat,

the secret police. One of them – the *ghassaleh*, a machine based on a washing-machine drum in which the victim's arms are inserted – had clearly made an unforgettable impression.

The businessmen sent for a colleague, and shortly a squat, round man with crinkly hair and turquoise eyes that contrasted oddly with his olive face arrived. Aptly, his name was Mohammad Al Azraq – Mohammad the Blue. He was headmaster of the local girls' *thenawiya*, or secondary school. He insisted on taking us to visit the grave of the great Arab philosopher-poet Abu al-Maari. The grave, which was sheltered picturesquely in a little courtyard by an ancient olive tree, was badly eroded. There was an inscription above it. Mr Al Azraq translated it thus: 'I die without issue. I would not do to others what my father did to me, for this world is naught but sadness.' Behind the grave was a gloomy room intended for use as a library by students. Mr Blue gestured for us to sit down and delivered this lecture:

'This town is called Maaret after the series of man-made and natural caves beneath it. There is a theory that Anuaman refers to Anuaman Basha, a king who ruled here once long ago. This town was destroyed by Tamburlaine. He burned it seven times and the earth here, it is black. Afterwards Tamburlaine went to Iraq, as you no doubt know, and he burned Baghdad so that the waters in the rivers ran black. The Ferangi [Franks] destroyed this town. They killed twenty thousand Moslem men and women and children but afterwards they are punished by starvation. They were dying of hunger and they ate the flesh of the dead people of our town. It is recorded in letters in the Vatican City. Then the Ottomans came. You can see the fine buildings they built. After the Ottomans came another occupation – the French one. As a result of the Syrian insurrections there were many casualties. But finally we gained the independence which ultimately brought our dearly loved President to the fore and his excellent Correctionist Movement. Since 1970 he has brought peace, education, stability and health to our land. He is a great man. Thank you.'

This spiel over, we were conducted to a cumin warehouse where we were handed over to an ugly boy called Mahmoud, who lived in the village of Babila. For a modest fee, Mr Azraq arranged for him to show us the dead cities of Ruweiha and Jeradeh.

At Babila, however, the pick-up we had been promised, and for which we had negotiated a fee, was in use elsewhere – in the Third

World there is always a heavy demand on transport. The only means of conveyance left to us was a stolid old tractor. Mahmoud jumped onto it. Rupert, Karim and I stood holding onto the mudguards and we set off at a snail's pace across the barren limestone wastes. *En route* we picked up a peasant woman carrying a large sack on her head and her daughter, who was carrying a can of milk.

Thus forming this social realist tableau, we continued our slow journey, crossing the trickle of the River Quaik and heading for the bleak, expansive and unyielding hills ahead. Here and there were little mines, with peasants scratching around in them, although what they could be extracting I could not imagine. The mother and daughter disembarked at Jeradeh, a pleasant village of limestone houses grouped around a core of Byzantine buildings – a tower, a church and several lovely villas with muscular grey columns in front of them. The toughness of the architecture of the dead cities was amazing. The lack of trees meant that everything – ceilings, balconies, benches, stairs and chairs – was carved out of lumps of sheer granite. This is the reason why so many of the buildings have survived earthquakes and the passing of the millennia.

From here it was a climb of a few kilometres to Ruweiha across an increasingly disheartening landscape of positively lunar desolation. All around us were great twisted lumps of grey limestone. As we chugged up the hill, we passed on our right an extensive necropolis. Many of the tombs had been cracked open – presumably by earthquakes – as though the Day of Judgement had been and gone. All were long empty. One mighty sarcophagus stood high on a crumbling plinth – a huge, plain, austere grey granite chest which rang out hollowly if you struck it with a stone. The top was askew and, standing on poor Mahmoud's shoulders, I glimpsed at the bottom a few scattered bones, pathetic in relation to the imposing charnel house in which they lay. I have never experienced such a feeling, not of death, which implies life, but of deadness as I did there on the massif of Belus. It is like going to the Moon and finding an encampment abandoned by androids.

No one really knows why the dead cities were built and why they were apparently abandoned after only a few hundred years. One theory is that they were the result of a population explosion that forced people to build on the barren limestone massif and cultivate what pockets of earth they could find by growing olives. In many towns you can still see the old olive oil presses, also made of limestone. It is believed that a flourishing olive oil trade emerged in these uplands, supplying the eastern Mediterranean via Antioch.

From Ruweiha we shuddered off into the dying light. Suddenly, as we rounded a corner and entered the next valley, the landscape changed completely to one of rich red fields dotted symmetrically with olive trees and newly planted corn and maize. In Dana there was a particularly beautiful tomb with a pyramidal roof standing by the edge of a field. It was Christian, dating from the third century, although the style was purely pagan. The cultural synthesis was intriguing: a pagan architectural form enshrining a new ideology in a village that had bowed to yet another ideological revolution and was now Moslem. It made me feel distinctly transient. This tomb had seen the rise of three separate belief systems and would in all probability still be standing long after I had been despatched into my own little sepulchre.

That evening we visited Baby Shoes' friend George in his flat in Suleymania, an Armenian district full of gold shops. George was half Lebanese and half Armenian. He was plump and soft-featured and very emotional. His displays of affection towards Baby Shoes were touching to witness. He ran a design business ripping off Western images (Mickey Mouse, various pop groups, James Dean, and so on) and turning them into transfers for bags, calendars, clothes and pencil cases.

We settled down to smoke the hubble-bubble and listen to John Lee Hooker tapes. Karim padded about the rambling apartment setting up the water pipes as he had been taught by his father. He loved George's flat which, with its posters of Marilyn Monroe and photographs of George's German girlfriend, was practically another country for him. From then on, much to George's chagrin and possibly Rupert's, he looked up to George, and availed himself of every opportunity to visit, or simply mention his name.

George was an obliging tutor in the art of *argileh* smoking, showing us how to make the different parts of the pipe airtight. He chose an apple-scented tobacco, and was very particular about teaching us the etiquette of the hubble-bubble. 'First, in Arabic we say that we drink a pipe. We do not smoke it as you in England do. For this reason we also use the verb to drink when we talk of the cigarette. In Arabic we drink cigarettes. Secondly, if you are sharing a pipe, you must never pass it with the mouthpiece pointing directly at the person you are giving it to. This is considered very offensive. You must fold it over so' – he tucked the mouthpiece back onto the lambskin pipe – 'and then hand it on. Thirdly, you must never put the water bottle on the table, thus obstructing the view of your fellow smokers. Finally you must never, *never*, light your cigarette from the charcoal on top of the pipe. It is *shame*.'

When we left George's flat, Rupert, Karim, Baby Shoes and I went to a sandwich shop near by. Baby Shoes told me about his curiously named friend Gladys, a jewellery designer who used to live in New York. 'You must meet her. Here, I give you her number. She loves Westerners. She go crazy for you. Gladys, she something very unique and special.'

As we entered the shop we passed a small Turcoman boy sitting on the ground. He was about six or seven years old and had placed a set of bathroom scales in front of him. Occasionally someone stood on them and tossed him a coin. When we came out again he was still there. It was about eleven o'clock and the boy, who was propped against a tree trunk, had fallen fast asleep. I stood on the scales. To my surprise my weight had plummeted. I put a twenty-five-pound note on the boy's grubby sleeve. His eyes were closed behind long feathery lashes. 'Take this,' I said in Arabic. Karim cuffed him gently round the head and the boy stirred. His green eyes opened briefly and he stuffed the note up his sleeve, almost instantly falling asleep again, his head rolling onto his chest.

Back at the hotel I could not get this pathetic spectacle out of my head. I had a sudden compulsion to go back. I would find out about this little vagrant. Maybe I could give him some more money, sort him out a bed for the night, adopt him. All those stupid, unrealistic things that tourists think. I left the hotel. It was bitingly cold. I flagged down a taxi and returned to the kebab shop in Suleymania. The urchin had disappeared.

6

Bassel, on Horseback

On the phone Gladys sounded exactly like Elaine Stritch. She said that she had to be downtown at noon to pick up a plane ticket (she was leaving for Paris in two days) and suggested dropping by my hotel in her car. I explained that as my hotel was in the middle of a street beleaguered by market stalls, dropping by was difficult. We agreed instead to meet at twelve outside the Baron.

I arrived at the appointed hour and peered along the street looking for Gladys, who appeared in a taxi with a large plastic sign affixed to its roof. In the back I could see a pop-eyed, grinning face with dark hair tied back in a ponytail and the sort of painted-on eyebrows that always remind me of a sad clown or Edith Piaf.

I got in and Gladys shook my hand. She was wearing jeans and a checked shirt, and round her neck hung a gold cross, instantly singling her out as a Christian. She spoke in short, brutal, Hollywood-inflected sentences, explaining that after picking up her plane ticket (she was due to hold a jewellery exhibition in Paris) she had to go to her shop to arrange the flowers for an engagement party that evening. She would love to talk to me, however; if I liked, I could accompany her to the shop where we could talk over coffee. From this I gathered that Gladys, apart from being a jewellery designer, also owned a florist's. I was intrigued to see what a Syrian florist's would look like – somehow I could not imagine it.

Her flat (which she used as an office, living elsewhere) was in a private block in Salib, an upmarket Christian area of Aleppo. Inside we encountered a hive of activity. There was a clumsy Amazonian female with short blond frizzed-up hair jabbing gladioli around the roof of a rather twee model wishing well. This was Mireille. A slightly built woman (Tina) was coaxing ivy round the chain, from which was suspended a bucket covered in chrysanthemums. By far the most docile of the three acolytes was a small young man called

Mohammad, whom Gladys sent packing to the kitchen to make the coffee. The strange thing was that, once back in her little kingdom, Gladys's patina of Uncle Sam amiability faded like morning dew. Maybe the effort of being American was exhausting her. Now she was back in the hot seat, holding the reins, barking orders to the staff or down the phone, working to a deadline. Sitting on the sofa twiddling my thumbs, I wondered exactly why she had brought me to this remote bourgeois suburb. Perhaps it did something for her ego. My various attempts at polite conversation fell like stones. Eventually she responded when I asked why she had left New York.

'For six years I ran a flower shop in downtown Manhattan,' she said, sinking carnations into a piece of green sponge. 'I loved Manhattan. But know something?' I shook my head mutely from the sofa. 'I didn't want to spend my whole life working. There were four people in that shop – two of them had AIDS. That's fifty per cent of the workforce, Robert. People spent two hours getting to work and two hours getting back. That's New York. All they do is work. So I came back. And you know what I noticed? There was so much noise. Everywhere I went I noticed noise. From dawn to dusk, nothing but noise, noise, noise. It was more noisy than New York.'

I asked her what it was like living in Aleppo as a Christian. She directed a withering look at me, as if to say: Don't come that old divisive chestnut with me.

'I'll tell you in one word what it's like: *excellent*. Say, how long you staying here anyway?' She suddenly sounded impatient, so much so that I wasn't sure whether she meant on her premises or in the country.

'Oh, a few months, I expect,' I said vaguely.

'It'll get hot,' she warned.

'How hot?'

'Hot,' she growled, like Louis Armstrong. 'And I tell you one thing, it gets so hot, you gotta get a hat.'

'Do you wear a hat, Gladys?' I asked.

'No, I do not wear a hat,' she snapped.

'Why not?'

'The reason I do not wear a hat is because me, I'm Syrian. OK? You, you're English. You don't wear a hat and you're in big trouble, sunshine. Got it?'

Having left Gladys, I flagged down a taxi and headed back to Telal, to Baby Shoes' flat. We were going to visit a state sculptor who was working on a double-life-size statue of the President's late son, Bassel, on horseback. Baby Shoes had to photograph the work-in-progress. As we were late, we took a taxi to a forlorn area on the outskirts of the city which held out the promise of burgeoning into an industrial estate. The taxi turned down an unmade rubble track in the direction of something large, square, concrete and unbeautiful resembling a nuclear bunker. This was destined to be the new art college of Aleppo.

The door was locked and we tiptoed round the uneven rubble precincts hallooing the sculptor until a responding cry came back to us. A rusty metal door swung open and we tramped down a cold, dusty corridor, turning into a very large studio, empty save for a colossal sculpture of a horse in full gallop. It was surrounded by scaffolding, and a man was standing underneath it, slapping handfuls of wet dark brown clay onto its underbelly. The head and front legs were eerily swathed in plastic sheets. The figure of Bassel Al Assad was so far represented only by a tubular metal frame straddling the horse's back.

In the far corner of the studio was a slightly built man holding a piece of flaming newspaper next to the head of the President's son. This was the sculptor, and he was holding the paper thus to see what effect sun and shade would have on the gigantic head when it was *in situ* outside, where it was destined to stand in the middle of a busy roundabout. He had been told not to let the shadow cast by the harsh Syrian sun make the subject look too old, too ugly or too severe.

When I asked him if he had had any contact with the President, the artist looked alarmed. 'The President is too busy with other matters of state,' he replied via Baby Shoes, who was doing his best to translate. 'I am being briefed by officers in the Ministry of Culture who are aware of the President's wishes.'

As it had been decreed that Bassel should be depicted enjoying his favourite activity, horseriding, the sculptor was working from a series of photographs pinned on the wall, showing Bassel galloping over various jumps at equestrian events. The finished work, explained the artist proudly, would stand eight metres high in front of a colossal twenty-five-metre white concrete arch 'signifying infinity and adorned with stars and shapes inspired by the Arabic script'. On a nearby table there was a scaled-down model of the sculpture as it would appear when completed. The arch looked like the jawbone of an almighty whale, the horse and rider as inconspicuous as a footling chess piece in comparison.

Bassel had, as far as I could tell from my enquiries, been a genuinely loved scion of the Assad dynasty, not least because of his good looks and dashing cavalier air. He had been groomed for a job that it now looked might well go to his uncle, the President's brother, Rifaat, a frightening figure who had long been seen as a loose and unpredictable cannon on the Syrian decks. In the early eighties Syria had come to the brink of civil war when Rifaat had assembled various army units on the roads leading into Damascus. There was no battle; Rifaat was outmanoeuvred by his brother and subsequently exiled, although he was later recalled and now held office again.

Twelve months prior to my arrival, Bassel had been killed when the car he was driving to the airport had wrapped itself around a tree. Ever since that day every available public space – shop windows, market stalls, lamp-posts – had been smothered with images of the dead young man. In the souk you could buy cloth by the metre, so cheap it was practically free, entirely covered with pictures of Bassel, or of his father (oh yes, in Syria, joke the people, there is a choice), to string up around your front room to earn Brownie points.

I had once met a German tourist over breakfast in the Baron Hotel. He said that for Syrians not to have a picture of the President or his son in their homes would be like a German family before the war not displaying a portrait of Hitler. It was simply asking for trouble, and whatever your sympathies might be, in a police state the last thing you wanted to do was draw attention to yourself.

Baby Shoes bobbed about taking photographs of the great work-in-progress and we were soon free to leave. It had not been a very inspiring visit. As we trudged through the sticky red earth towards the road, I reflected that this Gorgon-like transubstantiation of flesh into stone would not be a rewarding or a cathartic one for an artist. It was merely the hewing of a ponderous, joyless, overblown colossus from the rock of subservience, and probably nobody – save a few Baathist dinosaurs – was ever going to admire it. When I said as much to Baby Shoes he laughed. 'Not rewarding? You know how much this man gets for this sculpture? Ten million Syrian pounds.'

Ten million pounds. I converted it into sterling – about 150 grand, in a country where the average wage was fifteen dollars a week. So that was where the money went.

7

The Almond's Heart

I was glad to get back to the hotel, just to be on my own and lie down for a while. Darkness had fallen outside. I lit my stove, then wandered into reception. Kamal had made me a cup of tea flavoured with sage and sugar. Funny to think that the secret police should make one tea. As usual the TV was blaring away at no one in particular. A fantastically elegant blonde woman in a floor-length eau de Nil evening gown was singing one of those long, anguished Arabic laments. She was middle-aged and had high cheekbones and a long face. Perhaps her family had been Circassian in origin. She was obviously a natural blonde and would not have looked out of place on a Nuremberg balcony next to the Fuhrer. For a moment Kamal and I both got lost in her wailing melody.

'What's she saying?' I asked.

Kamal thought for a moment. 'She say, "You are happy for you can forget. I am sad for I cannot forget".'

'Is that all?'

'Yes. It is all.'

'But what about all the other words?' The song had been going on for ages.

'There are no other words. We like the words so we sing them again and again.'

The song died away, leaving me with a hollow feeling in the pit of my stomach. There was ecstatic applause from the glitzy middle-aged audience – pot-bellied men in shiny suits, women with big hair and clip-on earrings, their jackets bristling with brass buttons and swollen with shoulder pads.

Kamal gave me a forced smile and said over-casually: 'Robert. Every day you come. You go. What you do every day? Where you go?'

I know your little game, you fat walrus, I thought. You make my
flesh creep. I said, 'Oh, I just visit friends, do a little sightseeing.'

'Which friend? Oris is your friend?'

'Not just Oris. There's George, and of course we mustn't forget
Gladys in the flower shop. Rupert, Karim. The people in the opera
company.'

I thought I might as well let him have all the details. None of these
people had anything to fear from the authorities, although it suddenly struck me that Rupert's frequent appearances in Syria might
look rather odd to the powers that be. They must be wondering what
he was up to. It then occurred to me to wonder for the first time
myself exactly what it was he was up to.

Later that evening Rupert popped in for a drink, plopping himself
down in the easy chair in my room. He looked crumpled, washed
out. In his collapsed state, with his waistcoat and porcelain-white
skin, he reminded me of a privileged but sickly Victorian child about
to be claimed by the ravages of TB. Only his predatory purple lips
looked dangerous.

'There's been a drama. It's that boy,' he sighed, absently revolving
his box of Omar Sharif cigarettes in his long fingers. 'He's run off
with George's cassette thingy. Or that's what they're saying.'

'Which boy?' I asked obtusely, handing him a tea glass of locally
made cherry brandy.

'Karim, of course. He cannot stop pestering George. Day in, day
out. Talking about him. Turning up at his flat and if he's out just
waiting. George says he only lent him the Walkman to get rid of him
and now Karim is refusing to give it back. When I tackled him he
burst into tears and said George had given it to him because he was
his new friend.'

I was about to make soothing noises when I remembered what I
wanted to ask him. 'Rupert, why exactly are you here? It can't be just
for Karim. Or is it?'

He looked startled that I should have diverted him from his
problem. He thought for a while, then said, 'Well, on the surface
maybe. But in all honesty it's not the real reason that propelled me
here. The real reason is that when I arrived here I sort of recognized
it. It was the land of the weak. The land of outsiders and outcasts,
where I am happiest. I'm at home here, in a strange sort of way. I
have a basic core sympathy with the Syrians: doubly outcast because

they're Arabs and former Soviet allies.' There was a ruminative pause. 'And, of course, I am homosexual.' He gulped his cherry brandy in one go, his arm shooting out for a refill.

It was a depressing response, but it struck a chord with me. I knew then why I had drifted into friendship with him. He was an outsider, a loner. I could smell it from a hundred paces precisely because I was one myself.

The next morning I had an appointment with George, who had promised to take me to a far-flung Byzantine church called Qalb Lozeh (the Heart of the Almond) on the remote northern extreme of the Belus massif. He was waiting for me outside the Amir Palace Hotel, looking pretty and fat and in a state of some agitation. We took a bus to the town of Harim, winding up into mountains even balder and greyer than those I had traversed in the vicinity of Ruweiha and Jeradeh. It was a fine, clear, crisp day, with a brilliant blue sky affording us endless views over the fertile green plain of Amuq to Iskanderun in Turkey, from whose border we were only a couple of hundred metres distant.

Throughout the journey George exercised himself about Karim. 'You know since that time you all came to my flat I have not had one minute of peace. That boy came to my flat *three* times yesterday and *twice* the day before that. Always he was admiring things, picking things up, saying how beautiful they were. You know how if some-one admires something in our culture then we *must* give it to them. He picked up my cassette player and said, "Oh, this is very nice." I told him it was far too expensive, pretending that I understood his comment was an offer to buy my Walkman. But now I cannot find it. It was very wrong of Rupert to bring this boy to our homes.' He looked at me. 'Do you trust Karim?'

'I really don't know him,' I said, 'so I can't speak personally.'

'Do you think he gains things from Rupert?'

'I think he gains cigarettes,' I replied.

'See! See!' exclaimed George victoriously. 'I was right! And if he takes a small thing like a cigarette then he will take a big thing too! You know it. You know it.'

Harim was a dozy, rustic, almost idyllic little place, thriving on olive trees and fish farms which one could see spread out in a patchwork in the valley below. But if any town had witnessed the upheavals of the centuries, it was this one. Its history was Syria's history, its fate, by and large, Syria's fate. In 959 it had been occupied by the Byzantines in their attempt to regain Syria from the Arabs. Nicephorus built a castle here in 1084. One year later the Seljuk Turks, a rising power, took it, ceding it in 1097 to the Crusaders, who wanted to protect the rearguard of their forces, then engaged in a nine-month siege of Antioch. Successive waves of Moslem and Christian forces occupied and reoccupied the castle until it finally fell to the Arabs in 1268. At the end of the thirteenth century the first of the Mongol invasions destroyed it and anything or anyone else in their path.

'I am going to take you to Abu Mohammad,' said George. 'He is my friend. He is from Lebanon and very poor but a very, very good man.'

Abu Mohammad ran a roadside kebab stall. He was stooping over a pan of charcoal in a dirty, ragged turban, griddling meat. Blue-grey smoke curled over the road and floated off into the distance. When he saw George, he rushed towards him, hugging and kissing him. He abandoned his stall and led us up some crude steps hewn into the side of the mountain to his house, which consisted of two buildings of local limestone at right angles to each other and between them a courtyard, dotted with rusty tins out of which roses and jasmine were growing. The roof of the first building had caved in, so we went into the second one, where mattresses covered in a garish floral motif were pulled out of a large niche in the wall for us to sit on. These were normally the family's beds. This room was where Abu Mohammad and his eight children relaxed, slept, ate, and where his progeny were conceived and born. There would soon be nine children, as became obvious when his wife was presented to us.

We were served tea and coffee at the same time – I had a glass of tea in my left hand and a tiny cup of coffee in my right. I had been force-fed an expensive Marlboro cigarette which Abu Mohammad had sent one of his bright-eyed boys to go and buy in honour of our arrival. It was sticking out of the corner of my mouth, the smoke making my eyes run, but I felt it would have been rude to have refused. Meanwhile the heavily pregnant Umm Mohammad had noticed that buttons had either fallen off or were about to fall off my coat, and had sent one of her daughters out to buy some navy blue cotton so that she could sew them on again. When I eventually put my coat on none of the buttons seemed to match up with the buttonholes, so that I presented a somewhat ruckled appearance, but it would have been churlish to complain.

The whole family seemed to be *en fête*. In the Arab world it is considered a compliment to visit someone, and these simple people had responded by giving us what little they could with a kind of uncomplicated generosity you rarely if ever come across in the West.

Back in the village we secured the services of a driver with a trezeena for what George considered the extortionate sum of two hundred Syrian pounds (four dollars). The trezeena is a humiliating, not to say dangerous, mode of conveyance constructed by welding a small two-wheeled pick-up-shaped platform and a passenger seat onto a motorcycle, the whole being generally painted bright red, blue or green and decorated with flowers, evil eyes and hearts. It is Syria's answer to the Robin Reliant. Ours had a black ostrich feather nodding over the front mudguard and a little cabin welded over the forward section into which we all – God knows how – managed to squeeze. I was virtually on the gearstick and the ride was painful. For the first time I envied George his plump buttocks.

We bounced off up the mountainside towards Qalb Lozeh, passing two dead cities on the way. The driver laughed and pointed at his engine, shouting above the din, '*Shughal Syria, shughal Syria!* [made in Syria]' The mountains were scattered with contorted lumps of grey stone, lying like dead seals and as barren as frozen lava, but the views were awesome. Eventually we came across a ruined Byzantine church standing forlornly amid stone houses, but we pressed onward and upward. The noisy gurgle of the trezeena startled a flight of goldfinches which stood out against the monochrome background like dabs of ochre, and we saw two hawks, a species which the driver told me was described in Arabic by the term *al losr*, 'the thief', a particularly appropriate name given their dramatic raiding activities. We trundled past a group of gaily clad village women who were taking large discs of flat bread out of the communal village oven – the *tannor*, a hole in the ground covered by a heap of stones. They were laying the pale circles on the rocks to cool. Horses ran free or were quartered in stables made from the old rocks that had formed the walls of grand Byzantine villas fifteen hundred years ago. On the brow of a distant hill stood a lonely and beautiful column which George said had once been the retreat of a hermit.

When we finally arrived at Qalb Lozeh I was at once impressed and dismayed. Dismayed because now the highest point of the

remote hillside hamlet was a modern water tower, but impressed by
the sheer scale and state of preservation of the ancient basilica before
us, the transepts of which still retained their flat roofs made of huge
limestone slabs. The main roof of the nave had decayed, being so
large as to have necessitated its being made of wood, a rare commod-
ity. There was an intact semi-domed stone roof above the altar
decorated with various strange motifs – swastikas (the sign of the sun
commonly found in Byzantine decorations and indeed used until
recent times in Syrian houses) and orthodox crosses. On the skyline
of the next hillside stood the jagged ruins of another dead city. We
had no time to explore further as darkness was approaching. We
bumped back along the track to Harim and miraculously arrived in
the town in time to catch a connecting bus to Aleppo.

That night Baby Shoes turned up at George's flat and the conversa-
tion turned to Gladys. 'Ah, Gladys. It is always "When I was in New
York I did this, when I was in New York it was like that",' laughed
Baby Shoes, 'but you know, she only lived there two years. Her
problem is she has no man. Well, sometimes there is one, but you
know, he is Lebanese and he fuck girl, he fuck boy, he fuck donkey.
He fuck anything.' I thought it a strange remark considering that
George, whose flat we were after all sitting in at the time, was himself
Lebanese.

I dawdled back to the hotel and stopped off to buy a bottle of
water at a little shop near the museum. It was called Boukein and on
the label it read: 'Boukein spring of 5,000 feet height. Natural fresh
water. The best to prepare baby's food and to conserve his teeth
healthy.'

As I dithered on a street corner, a young, academic-looking man
approached me and said, 'Excuse me, sir. May I help you? Perhaps
you require a hotel or a map?'

I replied that I had both and that I was looking for a local
restaurant, and besides I had a guidebook, albeit rather cursorily
written. The young man said that he worked for a new private tourist
company. 'So you must have seen this guidebook?' I asked.

The young man flinched and looked over his shoulder. He spoke
good if robotic and hopelessly outdated English. 'I have indeed seen
it. In fact this book which you are scrutinizing presently is banned by
our authorities. It is illegal for us to possess it.'

'Banned? Why?'

'It is banned because it contains anti-government information.'

He introduced himself, saying his name was Rachid, and that he had only just started working for the tourist office, providing free information and offering tourist programmes to travellers. He kept looking around furtively, and then said, 'I think perhaps it is better to come inside. You see, I do not wish to cause you any consternation, but it is against the law for us to talk to Europeans.'

This strange conversational gambit initiated my friendship with the young tour operator. He was intelligent and, as well as English, spoke German and some French and Russian. The latter he was learning from his Russian girlfriend. He tried to interest me in some of his city tours, taking in various aspects of Aleppo: its architecture, its different quarters – Armenian, Christian, Moslem, Assyrian, Kurdish, and so on. I asked him whether the tour included the old Jewish quarter. 'Initially, yes of course, we included this quarter. At one time the Jewish population of this town was quite large. Now it is reduced to a few families only. The Jewish area is a very old and interesting area but you would need a guide to find it as the Jews may not display any Jewish sign or information, and they may only practise their religion in their homes or in the synagogue. The tour which took in this area is now I am afraid permanently suspended. It soon came to the attention of the secret police, and it was made clear that I should drop this element from the programme.'

I wondered exactly how these things were 'made clear'.

'Do most people know who the Mukhabarat are?'

'Yes, generally it is well known. Members of the Party are normally the ones who carry guns. But we know who the Mukhabarat are too.'

I had occasionally noticed ordinary civilians who when, for example, paying for something in a shop might open their jackets to reveal a pistol in a holster. The first time I crossed the border into Syria, our bus was flagged down and a man in civilian clothes came down the bus and demanded our passports and papers. Everyone handed them over without a moment's hesitation. Later we passed a café and the secret policeman stopped the bus, got out and ten minutes later boarded it again with twelve pots of ice cream which he distributed among the passengers. To subscribe to an inhuman system does not necessarily mean you are evil.

According to Amnesty International there were eight different levels of secret police operating in Syria. I had glanced at Amnesty's reports in England and they made appalling reading. Many journalists seemed to have been languishing in jail for twenty or thirty years or more.

'There is only one request really made of us as a people and of anyone who comes to this country,' said Rachid. 'That is never to involve yourself in politics. Never speak badly of the President. Surely you are aware of these things?'

I replied that I was indeed aware of them.

'For example,' said Rachid, clearing his throat, 'what is your opinion of his esteemed excellency the President?'

Something in his tone made me nervous. I replied, 'I think the President is a highly competent and respected ruler.'

Rachid looked at me levelly. 'Quite. I am glad to see you share my opinion.'

That night, as I lay in bed, I thought of England. What a *soft* country it seemed in comparison, with its rich, dimpled green fields, its fat hedgerows, its temperate climate, its moderation, its lack of extremism, its freedom of speech. The young man who ran the kebab shop near the hotel had once said to me, 'In England you can criticize your Prime Minister and yet he will still give you money if you have no work. Why does he do this? Is he mad?' There was no concept of freedom of expression in Syria, or of a government being accountable to its people. Here people were accountable to the government, and you were never allowed to forget it. In all the months I had spent in Syria I do not think I had encountered one eccentric – mad people, perhaps, but no eccentrics. Eccentricity was another characteristic of a nation that was able to express itself in whatever way it chose.

I was drifting off to sleep. I remembered that Baby Shoes was sending his friend Tadeus to wake me at six o'clock. We had planned a trip to a remote monastery hanging off a cliff in central Syria. Dimly, I was aware of the pounding of the printing presses below sending shivers through the building. They were obviously hurrying to complete some late-night order. The relentless thud, thud was like a terrible chained creature stamping its feet. I could feel its distress through the mattress.

The Monastery of St Moses

I was woken from a nightmare by Kamal banging on the door with his meaty fist. He told me that my friend Mr Tadeus was waiting for me in reception. Bleary-eyed, I staggered out and registered Tadeus sitting on the sofa. He nodded. 'You coming to the monastery?' he asked. I nodded back. 'You should be ready by now. You better hurry.'

I dressed in an uncoordinated manner, experiencing that sense of nausea you get when you are brusquely roused from a deep sleep, and stumbled back into reception feeling like death. Kamal was plying Tadeus with questions. Even with my simpleton's Arabic, I could see that Tadeus was being evasive. As we went down the stairs, he said, 'That guy recognized me from a factory I worked in years ago. He was asking where we were going. What I was doing. Then he wanted my name. He kept saying, "I can't quite remember your name. I have it on the tip of my tongue. Just jog my memory." I think he was checking up on me.'

The monastery of St Moses – when we eventually got there a ghastly bus ride later – was indeed splendidly isolated, perched in the cleft between two mountains and gazing across a sandy plain that disappeared ultimately in a pearly grey haze. To get there our group – Baby Shoes, Tadeus, a Frenchman from the French Cultural Centre, an Algerian girl, Fatima, from the university, an Australian called Keith, and myself – had taken an overcrowded boiling-hot hop-hop to Nabk, a pick-up with no suspension into the mountains, and then, when the road petered out, we had shouldered our bags and walked along a wadi for thirty minutes under the midday sun.

At first sight the monastery, with its secretive slit windows, looked like an old fort, and I learned later that it was believed to have started life before the dawn of Christianity as a Roman watch tower. The door was diminutive and I grazed my back on it as we entered, remembering as I did so having been told about the doors in monasteries always being made deliberately small to remind the monks every time they passed through them how difficult it was to enter into paradise. 'Strait is the gate,' a biblical voice intoned in my head.

A Palestinian man greeted us and said that a service was in progress in the chapel which we were welcome to join. Outside the chapel door I noticed a heap of Western-style footwear in small sizes. I braced myself to encounter some reminder of contemporary existence, possibly a clutch of local children lisping their prayers. Inside the room was awash with the deep, dark colours of the ancient frescoes on the walls and the Persian rugs and kelims on the floor. Sitting cross-legged in a semicircle, with their backs to us, each on a fluffy white sheepskin as though perched on clouds, was a group of no fewer than six Japanese. I steadied myself against a nearby pillar, regarding this sight as a terrible intrusion and desperately trying to muster up some feelings of ecumenical goodwill. At the same time I was heartened to find lying stretched out on the rugs in the middle of the worshippers, in prime position before the rickety old stove, two long-haired cats, one black-and-white, the other tortoiseshell-and-white. I learned that they were called Abu Khallil and Umm Badia, and that they were very much in demand as lap-warmers in this priestly community. It became very cold at night and the monastery had little heating save for the extremely rusty stoves, and lighting only at prescribed times when the generator was switched on.

The service was being conducted by a corpulent bearded priest. His Arabic was pitted with all manner of splendid guttural sounds and glottal stops, so pronounced that they echoed around the chapel. He was Father Paolo dell'Oglio, an Italian Jesuit who had studied in Beirut and had ended up on this wild escarpment in the wilderness having heard about the monastery, abandoned for three hundred years, and tracking it down to see if it could be salvaged. Its on-going restoration was the subject of donations from the Vatican and the Italian and Syrian governments. Various art historians from Rome had worked on restoring the frescoes, giving of their time and skills free of charge.

Not understanding the service, I had plenty of opportunity to scrutinize the frescoes. The most dramatic was of the Last Judgement and covered the entire wall opposite the altar. It depicted various levels of hell; in the middle were the scales of good and evil attended by the Devil and an angel; at the top stood St Peter by the gate of heaven; right at the bottom, painted in a bold, naive style, was a bizarre group of naked prostitutes, each with their eyes, ears, nose or mouth penetrated by a black snake. A graphic warning to the illiterate of the punishment that awaited those who abused their bodily senses. In many of frescoes the figures appeared to have had their faces gouged out.

After the service I was introduced to Father Paolo. He took me around the church, pointing out how to distinguish a seventh-century fresco from a tenth-century one. He told me that about forty per cent had been lost in all, some partially removed in the sixties for sale, which explained the decapitated condition of so many of the figures. I wondered where all these heads were now. Probably somewhere in Europe or America, with faked provenances, gracing some captain of industry's downstairs loo.

Our party for dinner that evening consisted of one Jesuit, one Syrian Catholic, one Syrian Orthodox, one Moslem, one Armenian Christian (Baby Shoes), one Armenian Moslem (Tadeus), one French Catholic (the Frenchman), one Algerian-French Moslem (Fatima), one Welsh Calvinist-turned-pantheist (me), and one agnostic (Keith). The Zen Buddhists or Shinto-ites (who, it turned out, were all diplomats on language courses) had left after the service. I managed to bag one of the cats throughout the proceedings, while the other dispensed her favours indiscriminately across the group. Over dinner Keith described his travels in Syria identifying wild legumes, including one that he was hoping to introduce into Australia on account of its entirely subterranean breeding cycle. The hope was that it would be able to reproduce itself each year for sheep to feed on. His trips took him to many remote parts of Syria, where he stayed with the villagers and Bedouin people, whose customs, he said, had more or less survived. 'Their hospitality is amazing. I have been to villages where people actually wash your feet for you. But by God, if you cause them any offence or dishonour they will kill you.'

After the meal we were invited to sit and meditate in the chapel for an hour, or take up raffia work. The prospect of meditating in the freezing chapel being one I could not face, I had little hesitation in plumping for the raffia work. It was terribly fiddly and my hands were icy cold, making me impatient and bad-tempered. Fatima and the French cultural officer had chosen the same option, and settled down to a serene, contemplative couple of hours – mainly of each other, it seemed. It was interesting watching all the alliances form. Perhaps, I schemed, manipulating my coarse strands with no little frustration in the lamplight, I could form one with Tadeus.

The next morning I woke to find the men's dorm in which we had slept deserted. I had spent the most fearful night. One reason was that the stove kept erupting in clouds of black smoke like an old man going into a coughing fit over his pipe. Then I had drunk some water from the Roman cistern without putting it through the filter and suffered the consequences in the form of a number of trips to the latrine. This necessitated getting up, blundering about to find a candle, lighting it, going out onto the roof, locating the ladder, gingerly descending it, scuttling across the terrace overlooking the now moonlit plain, and disappearing up a rough-hewn staircase into the tower, where a squat loo was situated. All this in the biting cold and a howling wind. The third and most angst-inducing reason was enough to bring on the second cause of my disquiet just by thinking about it. I realized that I had failed to renew my visa and was thus in the country illegally.

I went out onto the roof and descended the ladder. Everything in the fine, thin morning light looked new, deserted and beautiful. There was no sign of human life anywhere. Occasionally I could hear the tinkle of a bell. Looking up, I could see the flock of goats with their floppy ears outlined against the sky high on the mountain. They were standing on the most precipitous crags, peering nervelessly down over the drop below. I watched them move up and down the mountain, marvelling at how they never lost their footing and moved so casually yet surely, nibbling the tufts of coarse, pale green grass that sprouted here and there among the pink-and-grey rocks.

I found Tadeus in the library and told him my tale of woe concerning the visa. 'You have to go back immediately,' he said, looking alarmed. 'Or you could be in deep shit.' (I permitted myself a wry smile.) 'If you like, I will come with you.' He said he was bored with raffia work and had taken a dislike to the abbot and could not wait to go home.

I too had experienced enough deprivation. Palgrave, Doughty, Blunt and Burton, your reputations are safe from me, I thought, hastily packing my few things before meeting Tadeus by the doorway. If we hurried we could get the truck which came every three days with provisions and was, thankfully, calling that morning. I went to say goodbye to Father Paolo and thanked him for allowing me to stay, adding that I had to curtail my visit 'for visa reasons'. He said I could come back whenever I was passing, which, it struck me, would not be all that frequently. As I left I stuffed a handful of dollars into the donations box. They were for Abu Khallil and Umm Badia.

9

Mohammad

The train journey from Aleppo to Lattakia is probably the most beautiful you can make in Syria. Having missed the early morning express, I caught the slow train which left shortly afterwards. It was packed with students and took simply hours. The views from the window were charming. We passed over valleys studded with fields and orchards, with lone cypress trees standing sentinel near by; we wound around mountains with little terrace farms and olive trees hugging their sides, and occasionally disappeared into long dark tunnels beneath them. The landscape was rich in cultivation. I saw a farmer in a baggy *shalwaar* driving a plough pulled by two brown cattle with long horns between twisted olive trees, while his wife, dressed in bright blue with a pink headscarf, stooped, planting the furrows.

To my surprise, I had renewed my visa without any problems, although the process had been baroque, to put it mildly. I was now free to travel for a further two months. The students and I started talking. They said that the mountains were mainly populated by Christians and Alouites. By tradition it was the Alouites who occupied the upper slopes, while the Christians occupied the lower parts. The Alouites, they said, always liked to be high up, as was evidenced by their white-domed shrines which could be seen on top of most of the peaks.

One student, Mohammad, was a dashing young man with dark brown wavy hair, long at the front and short at the back. He had a fine, long, olive-skinned face with high cheekbones and brown eyes flecked with amber. He wore beautifully tailored navy blue slacks and a shell-pink shirt and dark blue cravat. He looked like a young Spanish aristocrat. He was studying English and his friends – among them another two Mohammads – law. They were returning home after exams. Like many students, they lived and studied at home, coming into town for a few days a week for tutorials and exams and staying in local hotels. I asked them for the address of a cheap but clean hotel, and when we arrived Mohammad took me to a taxi, gave orders to the driver and said he would meet me at the hotel, the Badia, that evening at seven o'clock.

The taxi drove through the wide streets. Nearly all Syrians love Lattakia, and all Lattakians believe they are a cut above most other Syrians. This is partly because it is the town nearest the President's village, Qadaha, but mainly because, as a port facing Europe, it has a peculiarly Mediterranean air. Strangely, the centre – still laid out on the Roman plan – is the densest, most cramped, most ramshackle and most unglamorous part of the town.

Lattakia began life as a Phoenician fishing village around 1000 BC, and in succession was taken by the Assyrians, the Persians and then the Greeks under Alexander. In about 311 BC the Seleucid Greeks named it Loadicea (hence the present name) after the mother of the Byzantine emperor Seleucus I. Mark Antony, during his shuttles to and from Egypt to see Cleopatra, granted it autonomy and reduced its taxes. It is mentioned in the New Testament, and St Peter passed through with his retinue. Around the time of the second century AD the Byzantine Emperor made it the capital of Syria. Subsequently the Byzantines lost it to the Arabs who lost it to the Turks who lost it to the Crusaders. In 1188 Saladin took it, and the Moslems held it until the Mongol invasion of 1260, as a result of which it was transferred back to the Christian Prince of Antioch. Worn out with history, under the Ottomans it shrivelled into a ruin with a silted-up harbour. Only when the French arrived in the 1920s did it receive a revivifying facelift.

Given this constant battering by invaders, it is not entirely surprising that Lattakia presents a thoroughly modern appearance in which hardly anything of the past is still standing, although there is much to be found underground. On my first evening's stroll I saw a pair of Roman columns being heaved out of the ground as a result of roadworks. The legacy of all this upheaval is a town with a special talent for adapting and using what has come its somewhat promiscuous way. Today, with its long boulevards lined with modern blocks of flats sporting large balconies, built by the French, it could be any contemporary Mediterranean town, peppered as it is by numerous boutiques, cafés and brasseries which the Lattakians love to frequent.

Lattakian women are famously beautiful and dress extravagantly, as close to the Parisian model – whether classical or trendy – as they can. They have wonderful cascades of thick dark hair, pale skin, a taste for dramatic colours in lipstick and fantastic costume jewellery. Lattakia was the only place in Syria where I saw women wearing miniskirts.

The town boasts two corniches, and I always confused them. The modern one was wide and long and sweeping, crowded every evening with the young and beautiful and the young and beautifuls' mothers. Men would stroll along arm in arm, ogling the girls. Rupert had told me that at night parts of the corniche were littered with young men hungrily seeking out each others' company. To find myself in Lattakia was suddenly to find myself in a more relaxing environment where pleasure was sought and found, and where it was a feature of the local economy to provide it.

The Hotel Badia was located on the third floor of a block in a square opposite the Ugarit cinema. It was so primitive it did not even possess a sign in English. I asked the taxi driver to wait and raced up the stairs to inspect it. I needed only a peek in reception to realize that it would lack even the most spartan comforts. The taxi driver said he knew a nice hotel on the corniche which was very reasonable. It was called the Safwan and overlooked the town hall, whose garden was dotted with the Roman statues that were unearthed every time the road was dug up. For only five pounds a night I got a room for three with a balcony and an *en suite* bathroom of a standard noticeably higher than that at the Rose of Aleppo – but then I was paying all of two pounds a night extra. I returned to the Badia at the appointed hour but Mohammad failed to show up. I left a note for him with my new address on it.

The next morning there was a knock on my door at about eight o'clock. I opened it to find standing before me a tall, well-built, prematurely greying man in his mid-thirties with striking green eyes. 'Good morning,' he said. 'My name is Mohammad and I have received your note from the Hotel Badia.'

'There must have been some mistake,' I replied.

'Yes. So I see. I was expecting you to be my friend Robert from Oxford who is professor of Akkadian languages.'

The confusion had arisen because the dim hotel concierge had given my note to a Mohammad who lived in a flat in the same block. This Mohammad clearly did have a friend called Robert, whom he presumed had arrived unannounced. He politely apologized, then suggested that we go out for breakfast.

We found a pleasant café on the corniche overlooking the sea and sat outside. All around us, well-dressed Syrian families were having breakfast before going off to work or school. Mohammad, it turned out, was now an architect, but in the past had worked extensively on various archaeological digs at Ras Shamra (the local name for Ugarit) and the Roman amphitheatre at Jebleh, just down the coast, as well as in the east of the country. He told me that it was well worth visiting Ugarit, the Phoenician town where the European alphabet had been invented, which, as a journalist, I felt I ought to do.

By Bronze Age standards, the remains at Ugarit are quite extensive. Most of them date from the fourteenth century BC and are remarkable for their construction in stone, whereas the contemporary cities of Mari and Ebla, having been built of mud brick, have not survived in anything like the same condition. Among the ruins was an acropolis with temples to Dagon and Baal – the Canaanite god – and a labyrinthine sequence of rooms belonging to the royal palace. One of these had yielded a great treasure trove of tablets inscribed mainly with the Ugaritic alphabet consisting of thirty cuneiform symbols, the first to equate a sound with a single sign. This was a great improvement on the previous system of depicting words by means of picture-based images, and its ease of expression led to its being taken up by the Greeks, who were trading partners, and thus it was handed down to us. The picture of life that emerged from these tablets helped provide historians with considerable insights into the Canaanite world, which several centuries later was to be colonized by the Israelites and make biblical history.

Like so many early Syrian archaeological sites, Ugarit could not be described as imposing, but it was in a peaceful rural setting surrounded by orange groves and with commanding views over to the sea and the long-defunct harbour, once the link between Babylon and the eastern Mediterranean. The remains of those houses still standing often had burial vaults beneath them, and the streets were characterized by stone channels that had once conducted water around the city. I was struck by the narrowness of the streets as compared with the grandeur of Hellenistic and Roman remains. Today I was the only person picking my way around the sleepy ruins, deserted save for the presence of a flock of long-eared goats which sent the stones rattling from the walls as they scrambled over them.

I took a taxi from Ugarit and rather extravagantly asked the driver to take me to Saladin's castle in the mountains outside the town.

Of all countries, Syria has the right to the title Land of Castles. There are castles from every period and every tradition, wonderful jewels in its architectural heritage. There are Crusader castles, Arab castles, Byzantine castles, Assassin castles, desert castles, mountain castles, some extraordinarily well preserved, some romantically desolate. Saladin's castle, described by Lawrence as 'the most sensational thing in castle building I have seen', is one of the latter. It is one of the most beautiful sights in Syria, built on a great tongue of rock between two green ravines with views beyond the mountain pass over the plain of Lattakia and as far as the sparkling Mediterranean. Today the spot is utterly deserted, the town that nestled in its enclosure for protection having long since disappeared. There is a spectacular road which winds up around the rock on which the castle sits, dreamily surveying its lonely rural domain. As the road nears the lower reaches of the building, it is cleft in two by a huge jagged lance of rock standing like a broken tooth, which eight hundred years ago used to support the drawbridge that passed over the sheer drop to the ravine below.

As I wandered through the keep, the donjons, the stables and the great halls, I noticed some tall, blond Europeans striding manfully over the ruins. They looked rather at home. The party consisted of an American, a Dutch student and two Australians who were kayaking their way along the world's great rivers and hoping to write a book about it. I found the idea of kayaking down the Euphrates an alarming one. What if you didn't realize you'd been swept over the border into Iraq? How do you even know if you're approaching a border when you're bobbing about in a kayak? It all sounded very risky.

Later that afternoon Mohammad II took me to the museum he used to work in. It was near the port and had once been a khan before becoming the house of the Governor of the Alouite State during the Mandate. There were some beautiful girls – real girls with thick chestnut hair, long painted nails, long eyelashes, honey-coloured eyes and glamorous clothes – floating around. One of them actually had a rose in her hair. They were so different from the dreary brides of art who habituate English art establishments. As we left, Mohammad said to me, 'Let me know if there is a girl you like. I can arrange something for you. The girls here are very free.'

That evening, after dinner with Mohammad and his wife, I traced my steps back along the corniche. It was getting late. I noticed a few lone figures dotted about on the benches in the park opposite the museum, and a constant drift of single men up and down the corniche. A young soldier in fatigues was lounging with a gun outside the police station.

A car drew up beside me and the window was wound down. 'Good evening,' said a fruity Syrian voice in English. 'How are you? You speak English?' A round face with bulging eyes was protruding out of the window. On the other side, behind the wheel, was a moody-looking man of about thirty with an open shirt and a very hairy chest. I confirmed that, being English, I could indeed speak English.

'You want come back with me and my friend? He want to give you coffee.'

They must think I'm a pushover, I thought.

The goitre-eyed passenger looked up at me coyly. 'You want threesome?'

'Certainly not,' I said in my primmest tones.

I walked down to the gardens where the cafés were and sat on a seat facing the sea to recover my composure. A tall youth in tight jeans and a leather jacket slouched past. He hesitated by a bench at the end of the path on which a lone figure sat, and then moved to a bench directly opposite. After a while he stood up, crossed the path and sat down next to the figure. Cigarettes were lit, a conversation started. A few minutes later the two men got up and strolled towards my seat in the shadows. The second youth was wearing smart navy blue slacks and a dark cravat. As they approached, he was talking to the leather-clad youth in a low voice, their heads close together, and a splash of lamplight fell across his handsome face. He looked like a young Spanish aristocrat.

10

The Island in Syria

The next morning I embarked on a full day of touring. As I left the hotel, the owner handed me a note that had been left the night before. 'I am Mohammad,' it read. 'I come to the Hotel Badia. They tell me you are in Hotel Safwan. I come at 11 o'clock p.m. and I wait for thirty minutes. Tomorrow I come again to see you.' That explains a lot, I reflected, perhaps a little sourly.

I sat on a bus to Tartus, waiting for it to fill up, getting more and more irritated the longer it took. The sweet lost-child's voice of Fairuz stole over the airwaves from the radio to soothe me. Now in her fifties, Fairuz still carries in her voice that unique freshness, that questing innocence which suits the Syrian mornings, before the afternoon heat blasts away the soft coolness. She is a goddess throughout the Arab world, quite simply adored by everyone, man, woman and child, in the Middle East. There is no equivalent in Western culture, where singers are divided by class or age. Fairuz unites the whole Arab-speaking world.

The bus ride was distinctly uncomfortable and cramped, not to mention painfully slow as we passed through Jebleh and the industrial town of Baniyas, bypassing one of Syria's most sombre and brooding castles, Qalaat Marqab, built of black stone and situated high on a rock keeping watch over the Mediterranean.

The old town of Tartus – or Tortosa, to use its Crusader name – is a wonderful crumbling rabbit warren of a place standing within the confines of the fortress. Its city walls, hugging it protectively against encroaching modernity, now seem maternal rather than defensive. Even the sea out of which they once loomed has retreated several yards down the beach. Today you can still find a tiny mosque built in what was one of the guard's rooms overlooking the sea, but most vestiges of the old fortress have long since been built over, on or around.

The lanes and alleys are so narrow, low and dense that it is impossible for an *ajnabee* (Westerner) not to stick out like a sore thumb. Housewives chatting with their neighbours and old men playing draughts in the cafés would stop whatever they were doing and stare at me slack-jawed. At one point I encountered a group of schoolchildren in their dark green quasi-military uniforms brushing the streets with red-bristled brooms. (On Fridays many children have to carry out community work such as this.) The children surged round me with cries of excitement and bore their find off in triumph to their teacher, who looked horrified that his charges should be consorting with such decadent company. One little girl publicly decorated me with a gold pin of the President's head. 'This is our President and we love him,' she cried. I thanked her for the gift and took a photograph of the group. As I raised my camera, I noticed that all the girls hung back while the boys thrust themselves forward, in line with Islamic principles decreeing that women should not be photographed. One large-limbed hobbledehoy cried out, 'Tell them in England the truth about our country. In Europe they say very bad things about our country and our President. Tell them it is not true. That we are good people.' In his own way he had a perfectly valid point. If we had the opportunity to stand in the Syrians' shoes we would understand more about the choices they have had to make.

Across the sea from Tartus is Syria's only island, now called Arwad, to which, in Phoenician, Roman and Greek times, the town always played second fiddle. The name Tartus in fact derives from this second-string status, being a corruption of the Roman Anti-Aradus, meaning the town opposite Aradus.

The ancient cathedral of Our Lady of Tortosa is one of the earliest known shrines to the Virgin, possibly established by St Peter himself as he passed through into Turkey. Today the building still impresses the visitor with its dreadful austerity. After fluctuating fortunes that have seen it used as a mosque and a barracks, it has, since independence, become a museum, and contains a veritable treasurehouse of unlabelled antiquities lying around in the gloom.

Today you can feel the fist of modern development battering against the frail walls of old Tartus with its inescapable series of ring roads, roundabouts and industrial buildings. It seems scarcely believable that this little town was the very last bastion of the mainland to be yielded up to the Moslems by the Crusaders. After two hundred years of war in the Latin Orient, or Outremer (the land beyond the sea), as the Crusaders themselves rather poetically called it, the knights quietly disappeared from Tartus over the waters to Arwad, taking the famous icon of Our Lady with them. For another ten years they harassed the Moslems from the tiny island, eventually, when all hope of re-establishing themselves was exhausted, withdrawing to Cyprus.

After my stroll through the town I took a boat across a choppy sea to Arwad, home to four thousand people. It is still crowned by a Crusader fortress and in the harbour the remains of the ancient Phoenician walls are still standing. Most of the time they are submerged beneath the waves, but when the sea is low it reveals a great lacy curtain of rocks, thousands of years of erosion having given them the texture of birds' bones, the huge slabs tessellated with a filigree of hollowed-out holes. Scattered along the promenade, lying on sheets on the ground, were crude souvenirs made by the locals. They were garish and tacky – wooden ships, fish and stars encrusted with shells and pebbles painted bright pink, yellow and blue.

After visiting the castle, I went back to the waterfront, found a café and sat down. I noticed a small boy staggering into the kitchen behind me, carrying a heavy bucket which he dropped with a thud onto the floor. Inside was a clod of houmous. Next to it stood another bucket of houmous, which was nearly empty. The boy stuck his hand into the sand-coloured goo and extracted a lump of it, flicking it into the first bucket and shaking his hand to dislodge as much as possible. Then he inverted the bucket and started scraping the remains out with his fingernails. I could hear it landing in the bucket with a splat. It turned my stomach. That was that. I could never eat houmous again. The choice of food in Syria is already palate-jadingly limited (unless you dine in a private middle- or upper-class residence), and to have to cross a staple element of the diet off one's list was galling. What was left? Falafels? Chicken on the spit?

The waiter arrived. I ordered a glass of tea. He enquired whether I would be requiring anything to eat. I replied that I would not be eating, thank you.

Two youths strolled along the promenade and sat opposite me. One, who had prominent spots, said he was a university student visiting his uncle. It was Friday, and the mosque was broadcasting its sermon across the island. It sounded like quite a rant. After it ended, the boy, who was called Samir, pointed out a squat, bearded man with red hair in the middle of the crowd emerging from the mosque.

'That is the village sheikh,' he said. 'He is twenty-eight and he studied law at Damascus.' The man was wearing a long white djellabah and a white skullcap. It was he who had given the sermon. 'That man is very important on the island,' said Samir. 'If there is anyone who has done something bad, this man can shame him in the mosque and then everyone on the island will scorn him.'

I did not fancy the idea of my misdeeds being trumpeted around the island through the mosque's loudspeakers, and the information rather blighted my appreciation of this picturesque spot. I imagined a straitened life in a little house at the end of one of the narrow, twisting alleyways, a life of Lorca-esque exposure to the pervasive inquisitiveness and need for conformity of one's small-minded neighbours. How many times a week were you sleeping with your wife? Why had she not conceived a child? Why were you arguing night in, night out?

Samir said he had been lucky as he had an Italian girlfriend and she had invited him to Naples for a holiday. For many Arabs the word girlfriend seems to imply almost any woman outside the family with whom they have a nodding social acquaintance. He must have been very well connected, I reflected, to have secured a tourist visa to Europe. His trip had made a tremendous impression on him. He seemed to regard Islam as a retrograde influence, holding his country back from developing into a modern state. The particular novelty of Italy was that 'you could utter your opinion and no one would arrest you'. He longed to live in Europe, he said, where he was sure he would do well.

Then came the inevitable girlfriend question. How many did I have? he asked, as if every *ajnabee* ran an unofficial harem with a selection of types to satisfy every whim. It was impossible to have sexual relations with a girl anywhere in Syria, he continued, unless you belonged to the class of rich internationalists, in which case you could do anything you wanted, including having your hymen replaced in Harley Street. It was particularly difficult on the island. 'You can have a girlfriend, but by girlfriend we do not mean the same as you in Europe. I have a friend. He is very handsome and rich. He is an engineer. He earns three hundred dollars a month. It is a lot in Syria. He tells me he has many girlfriends. Sometimes he has sex. Well, in a manner of speaking. You can only go so far. You see, you can never have penetration.'

'If a girl is discovered not to be a virgin on marriage,' I asked, 'what will happen to her?'

'She will die.'

'At whose hand?'

'At her father's. Her husband's. Her brother's. It does not really matter which. But she will die at any rate.' He laughed uneasily.

'So how do you satisfy your sexual feelings if you are a young professional man in Syria and you don't have enough money to get married?'

'It is simple. We cannot.'

'Is there any homosexuality on the island?'

'Yes. There are many such men on the island. But I, I am not interested in such activity. And in fact I scorn such men. I scorn them. Besides, for this there is the death penalty. This crime is even worse than to take the virginity of a girl to whom you are not married.'

In fact the legal punishment for homosexuality was nothing like this extreme. Nevertheless, it all sounded pretty dire, and I was beginning to long for the next boat back. The sky had turned dark and stormy, the sea a steely grey. In the distance the ferry chugged into view. Samir walked me to the jetty where there was a rowdy gang of people who jostled each other and leapt on the boat before it had docked while others leapt off. It took a further three boats before I could embark, and by this time the sea was very rough.

'Goodbye, Mr Robert,' said Samir sweetly. 'Please write to me. Maybe we can meet in England.'

'Or maybe Italy,' I said jokingly.

'Yes. Both would be nice,' Samir replied solemnly. 'OK. So long. *Ciao*.'

The crossing back was nerve-racking. The boat was positively weighed down with people and luggage. Some were sitting – somewhat unenviably – on the roof. The man standing next to me had been a sailor, and was teaching me how to stand with my knees slightly bent to resist the buffeting of the shiny black waves. I was relieved to regain the mainland.

11

Damascus

Partir, c'est toujours mourir un peu is a phrase we all instinctively understand. It does not, of course, mean that part of you dies, rather that you experience the dying passively, as a bereavement. The awareness of transience is scarcely ever brought home more poignantly than when travelling alone in a strange land. To travel is to be always to some extent in a state of bereavement, always to have somebody die on you a little. All the fellow passengers, the helpful pedestrians, the nice young men, the pretty girls, the kind families who took you in, the smiling hosts and hostesses – all of them swept ruthlessly, inexorably into oblivion with your passing.

These thoughts surged through my mind as relentlessly as the landscape rolled by the windows of the bus on which I was sitting, bound for Damascus, a considerable city of over three million inhabitants. I had felt irretrievably drawn to Damascus, like a shard to a magnet. Now I was being sucked into its epicentre in the most frightening way. 'Hang on, I didn't choose to do this,' part of me wanted to say. With each passing mile I contemplated the prospect with mounting dread. Here I was, about to face another great dollop of disorientation, hassle, confusion. As we started to cut through the mundane grey jerry-built suburbs, I found my brow beaded with a fine mist of sweat. Why was I putting myself through this mill?

But as the bus ploughed on into the centre, I found myself becoming filled with a sneaking curiosity, wanting to sense the city's intrigues and to penetrate its mysteries and particular rhythms. It was a sinister place, positively draped with images of its President. Some were airbrush paintings several storeys high, hung over complete fascias of buildings. Some were great plaques surrounded by clusters of flashing coloured lights. Others took the form of bunting, repetitive images of Warhol-like kitschness dancing and fluttering across the streets.

I was in the capital, the seat of the ruling Baath Party, the totalitarian Arab Marxist movement that had swept to power almost twenty-five years previously and brought to prominence the impoverished mountain-dwelling Alouis, a strange Shia sect whose mysterious rites denied them acceptance in majority Sunni society. This was the nerve centre of the Baath revolution. Here, emasculated, sat the grudging ranks of the old Sunni bourgeoisie, now obliged themselves to adulate the dynasty that had gelded them. Here too lodged all the Palestinian splinter groups, considered by some to be little more than terrorist cells, hunted out of every Arab state but this one; the President had welcomed every element that hated the neighbouring state that had robbed Syria of her sovereign territory – the Golan Heights – in 1967. Presumably somewhere too were representatives of the decimated Moslem Brotherhood, blasted out of existence by the tanks of the President's brother in 1982. I wondered in which grimy block of flats they lived, on which balcony they stood. A policeman chugged by on his motorbike. On his windscreen I counted six images of the President or his son. Was it *all* show, I wondered again, or was this clamouring obeisance a sign of something else, an unfulfilled desire in the hearts of the Syrian nation for a dynasty, the desperate yearning of frightened children for Big Daddy?

Getting off the bus, I took a taxi to the Al Haramein Hotel in Suk Sarouja, where I was rendezvousing with Rupert. It was only a couple of minutes before the driver stopped just past a hostile modern flyover, pointing to a series of steps descending from the road between two vast modern blocks. From where I stood it appeared to be the merest chink between the two buildings, but as I started down the steps I found the most welcoming of sights: a wonky street of terraced shops over-canopied with vines and creepers so that the light below was soft and dappled.

The Al Haramein was a charming old Damascan house. It cost three pounds a night for a bed in a shared room, more if you wanted a room to yourself. Inside there was a courtyard open to the sky, with a mother-of-pearl-inlaid sofa on a raised *liwan* (platform) at the end. In the middle was a marble basin matching the cool marble floor from which a fountain spurted. Three goldfish swam in the basin's crystal-clear water. Around the courtyard were palms and aspidistras. The wall tiles were of basalt, the doors of carved wood with tiny panes let into them. Above the sofa was a picture of a distinguished old man in a fez – the father of the present owner, who had purchased the house from a Turkish pasha. Later it had served as a training academy for French officers under the Mandate. It retained the welcome atmosphere of a private home gone slightly to seed.

I was standing on the *liwan* taking all this in when I heard the clatter of feet on the rickety wooden staircase. A pair of highly polished black brogues came into view, followed by a stylishly cut pair of pin-striped trousers. Above was a sharply tailored silk waistcoat from which burst a rustic Georgian linen shirt with frills down the front. It was Rupert, his hair brilliantined, smoking a cigarette in a black holder. 'Darling boy, I am *so glad* to see you. Let us find you a beautiful room immediately.'

He took me upstairs with the manager and suggested I choose a room at the back to avoid noise. I soon found one with a floor decorated with geometric stone tiles in black, brown and white, dotted with threadbare carpets. The bedsteads were of wrought iron and brass, and the window looked out onto the roof terrace which was covered with roses and jasmines growing in rusty tins. It was a very pleasing effect. Rupert poked his head out of the window to check that there were no loudspeakers from neighbouring mosques aimed at my bed – the curse of the traveller in the Middle East is the dawn call to prayer.

He had a single room on the ground floor. Over tea on the *liwan*, he told me that there were no Amex banking facilities in Damascus and as he was unable to draw cash from his account (he owed me six hundred dollars) he proposed 'a little trip to Disneyland'.

'Where?' I asked, confused.

'You know – *Disneyland*,' he said, raising his eyebrows. 'That country run by the Americans over the border.' He was referring, of course, to Israel, Disneyland being travellers' argot for the unmentionable state. The nearest Amex bank was in Jerusalem, and he was intending to leave that day and hopefully get back within the week.

After he had left to catch the bus to Amman, I remained on the *liwan*, trying to digest Sir Stephen Runciman's *History of the Crusades*. Sitting near by was a tall, burly, rather sad-looking Australian with blond hair who introduced himself as Greg. He look dazed and exhausted, a condition explained by the fact that he was battling against amoebic dysentery, which he presumed he had contracted in Harrem, where he had drunk unpurified water.

'It was terrible for the first two weeks. Everything went through me, the colour of water,' he told me, with the alacrity of the invalid obsessed by his symptoms. 'I went to the hospital and they gave me some antibiotics which helped a little but there's not much you can do. They told me to eat plain rice and yoghurt and nothing else. The problem is that there is very little plain rice to be found in Syria as most of it is cooked in oil or animal fat, and my stomach just can't take it.' He added that today there had been cause for celebration as – wonder of wonders – that very morning fortune had smiled upon him and he had broken wind, a fact, he felt, that presaged the return of nice firm stools. I congratulated him on the news, smiling as brightly as I could.

Greg had been in the hotel a week. Back home he had sold advertising space on the local rag in Alice Springs. Like many Australians he had an all-consuming mania for travelling, and had saved sufficient money to be able to live off the interest if he travelled wisely. In fact, according to his calculations, the Al Haramein was so cheap that he could stay there and eat plain rice and yoghurt to the end of his born days and still actually *save* money. He was in no hurry to leave.

Certainly there could be fewer more pleasant places in which to drift along. Although the hotel did not appear in any guidebooks, it always seemed to be full. The occupants were young, faintly alternative, gregarious and independent at the same time. I wholeheartedly approved of the establishment. It was how I imagined the hotels in Tangiers in which Paul and Jane Bowles, Burroughs and the Beat poets all hung out.

I drowsed on my bed, musing on my good fortune. I had a week to spend in a wonderful hotel in the heart of one of the most historic cities in the world. I decided then and there that I was not going to plan a thing.

Outside, a canary, imprisoned in a tiny cage, trilled its heart out, and I drifted into a blissful afternoon sleep in the city of Hafez Al Assad and St Paul.

12

The Perfume of Rosewater

It occurred to me that I could take up Caroline Sharman on her offer to see the rehearsals for *Dido and Aeneas*. I duly arranged to meet her and her costume designer, Angela Dodson, for breakfast. They were staying in a dreary 1970s hotel, the Damascus International, which, it turned out, was just round the corner from the Al Haramein. Breakfast was a brief affair as Angela was embarking on a foray to the Al Yarmuk camp on the outskirts of Damascus to visit a Palestinian workshop that had been commissioned to make the costumes for the production. I asked if I could accompany her, and we were duly whisked away in the British Council car which was waiting downstairs.

A long ribbon of Damascan suburb yawned before us, but after about half an hour we found ourselves driving through a bustling street market whose piles of green herbs and vegetables – coriander, parsley, mint, lettuce, cucumber – stood out brightly against the old brown buildings around them. At least, they looked old on account of the patina of dust and grime that encrusted them. On closer inspection they turned out to be made of breeze block and concrete, and most of them had clearly been constructed in the last few years. Every so often, little thoroughfares covered in webs of vines branched enticingly off the main street. Filled with an urge to explore, I asked the driver where we were. 'This is Yarmuk,' he replied to my surprise. We had arrived in the camp.

Yarmuk was given to the Palestinians by the Syrian government in 1948 on a hundred-year lease. Since then it has sprouted into a huge suburb of about one million people, of which only a quarter are now Palestinian. As a haven of intellectualism and political debate, it appeals to young professional couples who cannot afford central Damascan prices.

It was not easy to find the workshop, which had been set up by a determined German woman called Gunde Roumani who, as a student in Germany, had married a Palestinian. Eventually, after much reversing up and down alleyways, sending sloe-eyed boys as runners to scamper excitedly in front of the car asking the way, we located it at the end of a blind alley. Inside, we were confronted by a scene reminiscent of the Bayeux tapestry as a group of veiled women bent their heads over intricate embroidered panels.

Gunde took us through to the room where her collection of Palestinian costumes hung. The colour that preponderated was red, which, Gunde explained, symbolized womanhood and the significance of blood and its loss in the menstrual cycle. If a woman was unmarried the embroidery on her dress would be blue, a tradition exemplified by the robes of the Virgin Mary. In eastern Syria, in towns such as Hasseke, Assyrian Christian women wore blue dresses with a white rope belt to commemorate the Virgin. Blue was also the colour used to ward off the evil eye – another reason why it was appropriate for virgins. 'After her marriage, the woman would wear a red-embroidered garment,' explained Gunde. 'When she became a widow she had to take off her red dress and put on a blue one again. If she got married again she would be allowed to add some red patterns to her mainly blue-embroidered dress. The dress therefore would indicate the woman's social status and her past.'

Palestinian embroidery is geometrical, based on a series of styles that have been handed down from generation to generation. The fundamental patterns are locked into the subconscious of the women, to the extent that some of the embroideresses could look at an unfamiliar pattern on a dress from another village and go home and reproduce it faithfully. Gunde went on to explain the symbolism of the garments, which she had spent years trying to learn. Many of the motifs had names, such as 'moon' or 'ear of corn', although often there was no obvious connection between the name and the pattern on the dress. 'Moon', for example, is depicted by a cross, which in Canaanite times was the sign always found on images of the moon goddess Anat, over her navel, considered the source of all life and fertility. 'Palestinian embroidery has created its own delicate, aesthetic language over the millennia,' said Gunde, faintly donnishly. Since the struggle against Israel got under way, the motifs have become more politicized, the dresses identifying themselves with Palestine itself rather than individual villages. Gunde showed me dresses whose motifs depicted the Al Aqsa mosque, the Dome of the

Rock and patriotic Palestinian slogans. During the intifada she herself had been moved to design an 'intifada dress' showing youths standing around the Dome of the Rock firing stones from slings. In calligraphic Arabic around its edges were embroidered the words 'Jerusalem for ever' – Jerusalem being given its Arabic title, Al Quds, the Holy. The colours were red, white and green, those of the Palestinian flag. Only in the Middle East could a subject as seemingly marginal as embroidery be so enmeshed with politics.

Since the exodus of many Palestinians from their homeland in 1948, and the occupation by Israel of the West Bank in 1967, the Palestinian tradition of embroidery has – like so many of their cultural traditions – been almost fatally disrupted. Gunde had established this workshop to redeem the vanishing craft and restore a sense of self-respect and achievement to the pool of freelance embroiderers she employed. A feminist, she had named the workshop after Anat, the Canaanite mother of the gods. Gunde was a strong, practical woman who had no time for formality. She had worked tirelessly to establish her reputation, and her workshop was now a lifeline for several hundred women. Twice a year she organized fashion shows featuring traditional Palestinian clothes in Damascus, Amman and sometimes her native Germany.

She led us back into the workshop to examine her range of fabrics, and Angela produced a pile of sketches for the fifty or so costumes that needed to be made up for the opera production. They were based on a mixture of Phoenician, classical, traditional Syrian and modern Western designs. As she presented each one she would occasionally adapt it. 'This is Venus,' she said. 'As you can see, she's wearing a classical toga, but we're going to have to change it as Venus does not want to bare her shoulders. This is one of Dido's messengers. She's wearing running shorts but ignore that and substitute tracksuit bottoms.' (It turned out that the father of the girl playing the messenger would not allow his daughter to wear shorts.)

As an expert in Arab dress and traditions, Gunde was a useful member of the team, pointing out the cultural differences between East and West. Angela wanted the sailors to wear tattoos, but Gunde reminded her that it was mostly peasant women who wore tattoos in the Middle East – generally on their faces, where they were considered a mark of great beauty. In the end, Angela, who was aiming for as much cultural fusion as possible, decided to apply Western-style sailors' tattoos in traditional Middle Eastern henna.

The meeting over, Gunde led us back to the main road. She lived just round the corner in a small apartment to which she invited us and the rest of the opera group for dinner the following week. She flagged down a taxi and gave the driver instructions in her fluent Arabic. Before we got in, she said, 'By the way, the film festival starts tomorrow. Do you want to come to the first night?' I said I would love to, and agreed to meet her at the Cham Palace Hotel in the town centre the following evening.

Back in Damascus, I strolled through the Souk Al Hamidiyyah. The cavernous market is protected by a flimsy arched corrugated-iron roof erected in the nineteenth century and strafed by machinegun fire by the French during the uprisings against them after the Second World War. The sets below are spangled by coins of light falling from the bullet holes. Apart from a few tourist traps at the beginning, with stalls selling inlaid mother-of-pearl boxes and furniture and ornamental daggers, there was little here that was fake or meretricious. It was a faintly grimy, bustling, hard-working souk. Occasionally a troop of Iranian peasant women in billowing floor-length chadors would float across my path on their way to one of the Shiite shrines, clutching their veils between thumb and forefinger. Small boys walked up and down selling t-shirts, paper snakes and Marlboro cigarettes one by one from an opened packet. One boy offered me a stuffed eagle with collapsible wings for forty dollars. I passed an ice cream parlour whose presence was announced by the repetitive pounding of the gelatiers beating their man-sized mallets against the walls of the barrels in which the confection was made. All around there was a brisk, businesslike hum.

I spent the rest of the day and the whole of the next wandering around the old town, seeing the famous sites: Saladin's tomb, the Azem Palace, various quaint museums lodged in ravishing old houses. Many of the houses, their courtyards and fountains resembling those of my hotel, were still occupied, but mostly now divided up to provide accommodation for several families, and often very run down. Sometimes I got completely lost, and had to be extricated by patient guides who more often than not pressed me into taking tea with them. At the heart of the old city lay its most dazzling jewel, the Omayed mosque, encrusted with golden mosaics executed by Christian craftsmen and flanked by the mighty ruined portals of the Roman Temple of Jupiter.

One day a curious incident befell me. I was lost in one of the lanes behind the mosque and I stopped a boy to ask for directions to the museum of epigraphy. Two teenage girls came by, both wearing veils, so I was surprised that one of them should offer to help me find the museum. It is rare for an unmarried Moslem girl to walk with a foreign man in the street. The girl said her name was Wafa; she was sixteen and a student, and the smaller girl was her sister. She wore a loose trouser suit and her hair was completely covered by a lace-trimmed veil serrated round the edges and pinned under her chin. She had large, intense brown eyes and a full oval face.

The museum was located near by in a beautiful old house of black-and-white brickwork, but it was locked. 'Never mind. Perhaps you would like to see something else instead,' Wafa said. 'Would you like to see the Shiite shrine? It is very beautiful and is built by the Iranians.'

Normally it would not have occurred to me to visit a Shiite shrine, but I thought I could not go wrong with a veiled Moslem as my guide. Wafa's sister kept giggling and looking at the ground to avoid eye contact with me. They led me around the back of the Great Mosque where we came upon a modern onion-domed mosque built recently in the Iranian style. It made an interesting statement along-side the Omayed mosque, challenging the traditional Sunni supremacy in its values and style. Considerable chunks of the old city had been cleared to build it – or rather renovate it, as the original shrine was very old. This was partly to do with practicality and quite a lot to do with the President's paranoia. People said that Assad had used the redevelopment of the Shiite shrine as an opportunity to thin out the rabbit warren of streets surrounding the Omayed mosque which could have been used to harbour opposition activities, provid-ing an ideal site for an ambush.

Wafa told me that there was another beautiful shrine to Lady Zeinab, Mohammad's granddaughter, on the outskirts of Damascus, which had similarly been lavishly rebuilt in the modern Persian idiom. She confirmed that these Shiite tombs had been allowed to languish in a parlous state until the President came to power. I was at a loss to know quite where she stood in all this; it was difficult to tell whether she was Sunni or Shia. Soon, however, all was to be revealed.

Wafa and I stepped into the mosque, leaving our shoes with a doorman, and entered the prayer hall. Inside, it was a blaze of colour and light. The tiles, of varying blues, came from Isfahan; the ceiling was of cut mirror work, so that the revolving silver ceiling fans were picked up in each tiny segment and the light seemed to shimmer all around us. It was like standing in a room being fanned by a thousand butterflies. In the centre was an ornate tomb draped in green and gold. It was ostentatious, weird and magical – something you might expect to find at Eurodisney in the Arabian Nights room. It was surrounded by an ornamental grille behind which stood a tall plate-glass screen. Black-veiled women were gripping the bars of the grille and sliding up and down the glass, kissing it in adoration, like large, black, amorphous sea slugs moving slowly over a tank, feasting off lichen. They had no visible arms or legs; they were just things glued by the mouth to the glass walls. Every so often an attendant came along with a cloth to wipe the glass clean. As she moved along, another slow black shape crawled behind her, grazing in her wake.

The atmosphere inside the room was verging on the hysterical. Occasionally some of the women would break out into a high-pitched, protracted ululation. One plump woman in the group in front of us was going around squirting her companions with per-fume, which mingled with the rosewater characteristic of all Persian shrines. The air was positively heavy with it. She caught sight of us and, waddling in our direction, sprayed our wrists too. She was wearing a gold face visor and had come on a pilgrimage from the Gulf. The waddling combined with the yellow bill put me in mind of Mother Goose.

Wafa and I withdrew behind a pillar to watch. 'I'd love to take a photo,' I said.

'Yeah,' said Wafa, almost aggressively. 'Go on. Take one. Take one now. They won't know.'

This was not quite the sense of propriety I was expecting of a young Moslem girl. Suddenly, she turned to me and said, 'I have something I want to show you.' She opened a book she was carrying and produced a small paper bag. 'Here. You can see if you like.'

I opened the bag and took out a card in an envelope. 'Open it,' hissed Wafa, seeing me hesitate.

I opened it. Inside was a somewhat gooey picture of a good-look-ing cowboy kissing a fetching young cowgirl. It was the sort of thing you might have found in *Arena* in the seventies. She probably thinks it's ever so trendy, I thought. 'Very nice. Who's it for?' I asked, not really interested.

Wafa ignored my question. 'Not the card,' she whispered urgently. 'Look inside.'

I opened the card and something small and silver fell out onto the floor. I bent down to pick it up and could hardly believe my eyes: it was a crucifix. 'What are you doing with this?' I asked, sounding like a middle-aged matron finding a pubescent schoolboy in possession of a porn magazine. Of all the places a young Moslem girl could choose to show a Western man that she had bought a crucifix, a Shiite shrine surely had to be the most ill advised.

'Isn't it beautiful?' said Wafa, taking it from me.

'Wafa, for God's sake put it away now, before anyone sees us,' I implored her. I dreaded to think what would happen to her if someone saw the crucifix. A veiled Sunni apostate holding the cross to her breast by the tomb of a Shiite saint – she would probably get stoned, if she was lucky, and me with her.

'Please. Do you think we could go now?' I asked, and Wafa, looking slightly put out, quietly put the crucifix back in the cowboy card, replaced the card in her book and coolly led me out. As we left I wondered why she had brought me here to show me her treasure. Was she a masochist? Did she get a kick out of it? Was this the Syrian equivalent of adolescent rebellion?

At the gate her sister was waiting for us and we walked on. 'You see, I'm going to convert,' Wafa said. 'Last year I met a Canadian tourist here. He did not believe in anything. Only science. I could not understand that. He was the first person I met who was an atheist. But it made me question my beliefs.'

'Why do you prefer Christianity to Islam?' I suddenly became aware of the younger sister's eyes resting on me.

'It's OK,' said Wafa, reading my thoughts. 'She can't speak English. She doesn't know anything. Neither does my family. You know, I go to church near Bab Sharki. I walk there in my veil and I take it off inside. But I cannot tell you why I am converting. It is something you must feel inside.'

I was longing to talk to her about her experiences and how she managed to conceal her church-going activities, where she was going to convert and how freely she would be able to worship if she did, given that the death sentence was the punishment for apostasy. 'Look, why don't we sit down at this café for a while,' I suggested. 'I'd love to talk to you more about this.'

'Sorry, Robert,' she said. 'I too would love to, but you know this is a Moslem society. I cannot sit here with you unless I am going to marry you. We will have to keep on walking.'

It was already becoming quite difficult to ignore the disapproving glances that people were shooting at us, and I began to feel uncomfortable, not for myself but on behalf of Wafa. As we passed the khan of Al Assad Pasha, I stopped to look it up in my guidebook. A man approached us. He was polite, charming and helpful. In between describing the khan to me, he was speaking to Wafa in a calm voice. A look of alarm shot across her face.

'Please, Robert, can we move on now?' she begged. She would not tell me exactly what it was the man had said. 'Everyone thinks that I must have love for you because we are walking together. They are saying terrible things.'

As there was nowhere else available, we sat for a few minutes on the doorstep of a locked-up shop, a pair of social outcasts. An old man hobbled by and muttered under his breath in the most contemptuous tones. I wondered at the courage of this girl who was subjecting herself to this ignominious treatment just for the sake of a few minutes' conversation with a stranger. It was one of those moments when I realized that however much I loved the Arab world, my liking was indissolubly linked with my gender. By the time we got to Bab As Saghir I had had enough. 'Look, Wafa. It's been lovely to meet you but I have an appointment,' I lied.

'And I have to hurry home. Our father will be really angry with us, we are so late. You know, last year I took the Canadian man to our house. My father was furious with me. When the man left to go to his hotel he asked if I would go with him and my father wouldn't let me go. In the end, you know, he came too, following three steps behind us the whole way.'

I had no wish to incur her father's wrath, or for her to do so. We furtively exchanged addresses in the street. 'Please write to me, Robert. Don't forget me, will you?' she said plaintively. She turned on her heel and quickly moved off with her sister. They did not look back. Soon they were just a couple of white dots in the crowd, leaving me standing on the pavement feeling like a criminal.

I strolled back towards Sarouja. The area had been divided by two main roads, so I had to pick my way across dual and triple carriageways to find the rest of the old road. Near Martyrs Square was a livestock market. It was one of the most distressing sights I had seen for a long time. Everywhere I looked there were birds in cages so full that the occupants could barely move. Many of the cages had bars missing, and often some poor mite had its head sticking out, lacerated and denuded of feathers. There were chickens, turkeys, guinea fowl, ducks and endless cages of canaries, sparrows and parakeets. On the ground were tall chimney-shaped frames made of chicken wire, stacked with tortoises. The smell of bird shit and feathers was overpowering. One stall was a particularly tragic sight. It specialized in eagles, falcons and hawks, from fledglings to grown birds. The older birds had their legs shackled and stood on top of the juveniles' cages. Occasionally one would spread its wings and make a bid for freedom, only to get pulled up short by its rope and come crashing to the ground. When this happened the fat stallholder took a break from his hubble-bubble, leant over from his stool, picked up the rope, swung the bird like a dead weight in a sling, and hurled it back on top of the pile of cages. He told me they had all been caught in the desert. They were extremely cheap. In fact, alive, they were about a quarter of the price quoted me earlier for the stuffed eagle in the Souk Al Hamidiyyah. The young birds were the most expensive. It was a sickening sight, made all the more poignant by the magisterial glare of utter disdain that these haughty but humbled predators directed upon anyone in their vicinity.

I emerged from the market at the seamier end of Martyrs Square, sat down at the nearest café table and ordered a glass of tea, emphasizing the words '*shwayer zuker*' (little sugar) to prevent it arriving clogged with a bed of sodden crystals out of which the spoon would be rearing. At the next table there was a tough-looking character in his late twenties smoking a brand of local cigarette. He had a long bony face with pale brown wavy hair greased back from his forehead and slicked behind his ears. At first glance I spotted the unmistakable aura of the outsider about him – something detached, savage, brooding, burned out. I asked him for a light for my menthol cigarette. He spoke English quite well and seemed to understand even more. His name was Jihad and he was Palestinian. 'You see that.' He nodded at my earring. 'I had two like that. One in each ear – when I was a baby. Now if I have one they all say that guy wants fucking. It's all they think about here. They're a dirty lot. Take no offence. In Europe it's different, I know. But here …'

He told me that he had once grown his hair long like a hippie's and it had provoked the same reaction. 'Some people in the Middle

East – it doesn't matter who they are – they can have dirty minds. You be careful. The worst are the North Africans. Do not trust any of them.' He smiled, and I noticed that he had some teeth missing on one side of his mouth. He offered me a cigarette which I accepted. It tasted bitter and burned incredibly slowly and then went out. He told me that he had been born in the camp. I told him that I had been there and it was not such a bad place. He laughed, and said that he did not live there any more; now he lived in the Christian quarter of the old city. When I asked him what he did, he said, 'A little repairing. Watches, clocks, washing machines and stuff. Nothing.' He looked into the distance and fell silent, back in his own world.

I had to leave, so I went inside and settled both bills, anticipating with pleasure his surprise when he came to pay, and left with a wave. He gave me a casual mock salute in return, unsmiling, and went back to his smoking and his reverie. It had been another of those cursory, impressionistic traveller's encounters, and I did not expect to see him again. I was wrong.

13

Money from Iran

Back at the Al Haramein I ran into Greg. Fortune had blessed him with a stool that day. It was, he said, like a slice of Bird's custard. 'Oh, Greg,' I sighed happily. 'That's wonderful news. I couldn't be more pleased.'

Upstairs I found that someone had chucked a rucksack on the bed opposite mine. I tracked down its owner and pointed out that I had booked the whole room, and I would be grateful if he could relocate his belongings. He was an English teacher who was checking out Damascus with a view to working there for a year or so. I asked him what he thought of Syria. He replied that, apart from the fact that his taxi had driven him past a public execution the other day, it seemed a very nice, quiet, well-ordered place. (Public executions, I subsequently learned, tended to be reserved for crimes of high treason and took place in football stadiums to ensure maximum viewing capacity.) He had just returned from the north-eastern tip of the country where the Kurds lived and where, he said, they had chucked a bomb into the Tigris to stun the fish and had told him to choose one. I wondered if he was paranoid or just an angel of death. All this talk of bombs and hangings. Now the embassy was cautioning people not to visit the north-east because of the tension with neighbouring Turkey.

I went downstairs and rang a contact of Rupert's at the embassy. It occurred to me that in taking up Rupert's suggestion that I make contact, I could check out the latest situation with regard to the Kurds. He sounded a pleasant young man, and said he would drop round to my hotel later that evening.

I busied myself with the *Syrian Times*. One article read: 'The girls at the Martyrs' Daughters School have prepared a programme of various activities to mark the Silver Jubilee of the Correctionist Movement led by His Excellency President Hafez Assad. The programme includes a lecture about the achievements of the Correctionist Movement and a symposium on the Correctionist Movement, an artistic evening and Party contests. In Hassakeh, the Revolutionary Youths Union Secretariat met with the leadership of the student units where the programmes prepared for celebrating this glorious event were reviewed. At the Tishreen University in Lattakia there will be a literary evening organized by the poets and other men of letters in the city. It will include an intellectual seminar, under the title "The Correctionist Movement: the First 25 Years".' It all sounded very exciting.

The young diplomat was a likable fellow. He suggested we go and find something to eat in Martyrs Square. He asked me what my plans were, and I told him that I was a journalist travelling round the Middle East, writing the odd article, and that I wanted to stay on in Syria for a couple of months or more, but that I was also going to 'Disneyland' – or at least that part of it that was once Jordan, or Palestine, or whatever. In particular I wanted to go to the north-east border to see the old Roman bridge.

The diplomat did not think this was a very good idea at all because Turkey had recently invaded the Kurdish safe havens in northern Iraq in order to eradicate the PKK. 'You see, once you're across the Euphrates you're in a completely different country. Different people, clothes, dialect, attitudes, everything. The Syrians have hundreds of police and agents up there now. They are keeping very tight control on things because of the large Kurdish population in the area. I would not advise going there at present.'

The Kurds were sending their sons across the border to fight. Tadeus had told me that they bribed the guards to let them over and that they all had plans of where the mines had been laid between Turkey and Syria. Many Syrian soldiers were Kurdish themselves and were sympathetic.

'But what is going to happen if I do go?' I asked. 'They're hardly going to create an international incident, surely, at a time when they're trying to win Western approval?'

The young diplomat reflected. 'Let's see now. It's quite a long time since they "disappeared" anybody. In principle you can travel to the sights – which are crawling with narks anyway – and you'll be OK. But in your case, if they have any suspicion that you *are* a journalist, and they find you near the Iraqi border taking notes and photos, and you have lied about your occupation to get in ... well, you could be in a very difficult situation. You see, the point is that no one cares if you come here, interview the President and go away again, but the thing they really hate is if you are allowed to wander around and talk to ordinary people. They might be suspicious already. They could just be waiting for you to put a foot wrong.'

We strolled round the square discussing this likelihood. In fact we strolled round so many times I began to wonder if we were outside because the diplomat did not wish to discuss this subject in a restaurant where we might be overheard. We must have looked fairly conspicuous, because as we passed the same café for the third time a pimp approached us and asked if we were looking for girls.

'I'm sorry to be so gloomy,' said the diplomat. 'You see, I don't think things have changed very much when you consider the Party. The young ones may seem reasonable, but behind them there are all these Baath dinosaurs.

'I don't mean to put you off,' he concluded. 'I'm only doing my job. I tell you what. I'll make enquiries. Give me a ring in a few days and I'll tell you what the general opinion is.'

The next morning I was woken from a deep and welcome sleep by a sharp rap at my door, to be told that I was wanted on the telephone. It was the young diplomat, I assumed with a rundown on the situation in eastern Syria. Instead he asked, 'Do you know who Fathi Al Shakaki is?'

'Fatty Al Shakarky?' I echoed. 'What a wonderful name.'

'Well, you might be interested to know that it's just become available,' he retorted with glacial irony. 'He was the leader of Palestinian Islamic Jihad and he's just been assassinated.'

He went on to tell me that Shakaki had been killed in Malta, apparently by Mossad. 'The point is,' he said, 'PIJ are based here in Damascus and they have just appointed his successor. You could probably get an exclusive if you want. I think I'm right in saying you're the only journalist in town at the moment. Just thought I'd tip you off.'

'It's very kind of you to consider me,' I replied, 'but there are a couple of problems. One being that I'm an arts journalist and the other that I only have a sketchy knowledge of the PIJ. I really don't think I have the background to draw on for that sort of interview.'

'Don't worry. We can give you all that. Perhaps you can come to the office. About ten o'clock OK? We can talk then.'

I went for breakfast in the café three doors down from the hotel and ordered my favourite bean dish. I knew very little indeed about the PIJ, except that they were behind one or two of the suicide bus bombings in Israel over the past year. I wondered what the embassy wanted out of this proposed interview, or whether it really was just a favour. During our last conversation this guy had been warning me not to go sightseeing in north-eastern Syria. Now he was suggesting I look up a bunch of terrorists in a Damascan suburb. It didn't make sense.

I took a taxi to the embassy, which was a disappointing, flimsy modern building up the hill behind Umawiya Square, in the direction of the presidential palace. Here and there, loitering about the streets, trying to look as 'ordinary' as possible, were shifty-looking young men wearing polyester suits. It didn't take a genius to spot the guns slung around their waists. This was the presidential guards' attempt at 'low profile policing'.

I sat in a leather chair opposite my contact and lapped up my briefing. 'Now, the PIJ have no relations with the PLO and they are smaller than Hammas. They are highly motivated, geared almost exclusively to "operations". Unlike the FLP or the DFLP, who regard only armed settlers and armed units as targets, the PIJ consider all Israelis fair game. They were responsible for the Ramat Gan bombing and possibly the Beit Lial. The replacement is a man we know to be English-educated. He is called Ramadan Abdullah, but we suspect that this is a *nom de guerre*. If you get an interview, you will be fed their propaganda line along with the usual quantum leaps of logic and conspiracy theories. But you might ask them things like how do they gauge their support in the West Bank and what do they think it is. Do they expect support from Hezbollah. Money from Iran. If they are opposed to the Oslo Accords, what do they propose instead. What is the effect on the group now that the Israelis have lopped its head off. Are they close to Hammas. Any questions?'

I was up to 'lopped its head off ' in my notes. 'Yes. Why, if Syria is so implacably opposed to fundamentalism, are they here anyway?'

'Good question. They are here simply because no one else will have them. The Syrians are ambivalent about them because of their fundamentalist connections. However, they are allowed here as a gesture of support to the Palestinian movement, on condition that they do not proselytize or hold political meetings.'

'How am I going to get in touch with them?'

'They have – or had under Shakaki – a very good mechanism for receiving journalists. I'm sure it will be very easy if you ask your contacts. I don't think I want to use mine. I don't want this to be seen as something floated by the embassy. And I don't want to see anything you do before it's printed. I'm just trying to help you, you understand.'

I left feeling confident about my proposed meeting. The prospect of coming face to face with a terrorist was quite exciting. It would make a change from interviewing novelists, debauched earls and monomaniacs who collected things like corkscrews or toy soldiers, which was my usual fare. Later I told Peter Clark, director of the British Council, about the affair, and mentioned that I could not work out exactly why I had been summoned to the embassy. He replied phlegmatically: 'Oh, they do that sometimes. They would be using you as some kind of spy, I suppose.'

I did not pursue the interview.

14

Rising Rain

I found it hard to locate Gunde in the Cham Palace Hotel. It was a hive of activity, with journalists and film crews waiting to snatch soundbites and interviews with the luminaries of the Arab film world who were in residence. I went up to the press suite and found little paper notices pinned around the corridors, seemingly more as an afterthought than anything else, proclaiming the President's thoughts about art (he was himself, apparently, a former poet). 'Culture is the noblest need to mankind,' stated one. Another: 'All mankind's needs in life have limits. But the need for culture is limitless. President Hafez Al Assad.' I felt like substituting 'greed' for 'need' and 'power' for 'culture'. 'All mankind's greeds in life have limits. But the greed for power is limitless. President Hafez Al Assad.' That was more like it.

I eventually found Gunde talking to a long-haired man with whom we shared a taxi for the twenty-kilometre journey to the Ebla Cham conference centre for the festival opening. He was one of Gunde's neighbours in the camp who had once been a popular political singer. He started off singing songs about Palestine of which the government approved – all perfectly politically correct, as any jab at Israel was welcome. In due course his sympathies for the oppressed led to him writing and performing songs about the Kurdish people. This was considered far too near the knuckle. The government had no intention of stirring up Kurdish nationalist feeling given that the disputed borders of Kurdistan encroached on part of its own sovereign territory. But the Kurds, grateful that someone had at long last given voice to the plight in Syria, had virtually turned one of the singer's concerts into a political rally, and that had been the end of his career. Thereafter he was banned.

The Ebla Cham, a sinister, science-fiction-like place run by a difficult general who also happens to be the President's brother-in-law, stood like a lunar module in the middle of nowhere. As we approached, I could see a great triumphal gateway of stark white concrete, reminiscent of something in the fascist style of Hitler's Germany, illuminated in the darkness. From here there was a long floodlit driveway leading to a gigantic, stark modern hall, also floodlit, which one approached by walking up a ramp. Everyone was drifting up this ramp as though being sucked into H. G. Wells's time machine. At the top, black government Mercedes were banked up, having disgorged the Minister of Culture, Dr Najah al-Attar, and her retinue.

Inside the concert hall the *haute bourgeoisie* were out in force, the matrons sporting their Chanel and Versace suits in lime green and orange, scarlet and bright purple. They had stiff permed, back-combed hair, and their garments vied with each other over the number of rows of brass buttons they could squeeze on the front. They were carrying handbags on gold chains with gigantic buckles in large Vs or interlocking Cs to match their earrings. They all wore high heels with gold insets in the heel or adorned with gold bows and clips. The men wore shiny double-breasted suits and had that lardy, out-of-condition aura of spreading waistlines that good living in the Middle East generally predetermines. There was a smattering of Western diplomatic and cultural staff, including the British Council representative, Peter Clark. I sat next to a Malaysian man in a dog collar and a purple shirt who was the Vatican's representative in Damascus.

On the stage in front of us was the set of a town with a bicycle in front, illuminated by fluorescent tubes. Above it the number 25 was flashing in yellow. This I took to be a reference to the 'glorious occasion' of the Correctionist Movement's silver jubilee. On top of the proscenium arch was a picture of the President. The orchestra struck up and the dirge-like Syrian national anthem began. The curtains closed and a lone spotlight hit the President's photograph. Everyone stood up.

After this the Minister of Culture took to the podium and walked to a lectern surrounded by microphones. Dr al-Attar was a formidable and long-serving minister, famous for her wig. She launched into a very long ideological speech, the text of which was printed the next day in the festival newspaper. She began by saying that it was a pleasure to 'reciprocate opinion and experience in full freedom as in previous festivals'. After generalities about the importance of film, which could take art to the masses, she veered off onto a wild attack on Israel combined with effusions on the merits of the President as leader. Every time she mentioned his name (which she did four times) the spotlight somewhat comically zoomed from her up the curtain to rest on the President's photograph again until the frenzied applause subsided. 'Under the generous and continuous patronage of President HAFEZ AL ASSAD [applause and spotlight to photograph], emanating from his awareness and estimation of the role of cinematic art, Syrian cinema is gaining in significance, in giving vision to the masses: a vision which must be endowed with knowledge and enlightenment if it is to sustain a country in continuous confrontation with the ferocious cheating, eroding, land-grabbing, lying, international-law-defying Israeli enemy: an enemy ignoring the recommendations of international legal bodies to return our land for peace. We have said it aloud and now we say it again: FULL WITHDRAWAL FOR COMPREHENSIVE PEACE. WITHDRAWAL FROM THE GOLAN. WITHDRAWAL FROM SOUTHERN LEBANON. [Ecstatic applause.] Our march is presided over by our illustrious leader, His Excellency President HAFEZ AL ASSAD [more violent applause and spotlight on photograph], he who is the Courageous One, the Sword Bearer and the Pen Carrier. He is now as he has always been – consummate as statesman, agile as swordsman and infallible as our pen man. In the shadow of his sword we enjoy invincibility, and in that of his pen the wide-reaching enjoyment of nothing less than a Syrian Arab cultural renaissance. Through him Damascus has regained its glory as of old, so that today it has become a platform radiating with enlightenment.

'In the name of the President, HAFEZ AL ASSAD [riotous applause], patron of this festival, and on his behalf I say to you, "Cinema people, welcome!" Please trust us that you are in our eyes and hearts. Welcome to Damascus, your Damascus, the Damascus of all Arabs. Peace be upon you.'

Dr al-Attar then bustled across the platform and resumed her seat in the front row. Her speech had been the emotional high spot of the evening. The film that followed was called *Rising Rain*, a title that quite clearly proclaimed the content to be surreal. It concerned a famous author suffering from writer's block because he had become the lackey of the system – the fate of all artists in Syria, up to a point. It was fascinating for me to see how a contemporary young director chose to express himself under the present system, and I enjoyed the film, despite its depressing account of existence in Syria. Its vivid surrealism meant that I could at least try to interpret it, despite its being in Arabic. Later I met a well-known playwright who said: 'I do not think that it will be allowed to be shown here. It will be banned. It is very critical. Normally they only allow the film-makers to show these films outside the country.' This was all part of the cynicism of the system: allowing the film to be shown abroad so that the outside world would assume that there was a lot of artistic experimentation going on in Syria, whereas in fact this was not the case.

As we were filing out of the hall, I ran into Peter Clark, who, better than anyone, I thought, would know about artistic freedom in Syria. He explained that there was a system in place whereby the artist was 'licensed' by the government and was permitted to say certain things. It reminded me of Lear's 'all licensed fool' – the idea that you could get your message across to a temperamental despotic leader as long as you did it in a pleasing and clever way. The fool could often say more than the advisers. But there was a more sinister side: allowing a certain amount of criticism was the system's way of using the artists as a safety valve. I wondered how it would feel to know that your artistic message was being subtly manipulated like this in order to keep the Party more secure in the long run. It must have been very depressing.

As we returned to Damascus on the bus, Gunde told me a little about her life. Her husband had fought in the 1967 war on the side of Jordan, and after the defeat had spent five years in prison in Palestine before being driven into exile in Jordan. They met at college in Germany, where they were at film school. After their marriage they went to live in Chatila in the Lebanon, but were evacuated from their home in 1982 when, along with the rest of the camp, it was entirely destroyed. They went to Germany for a while, but their children (two daughters and a son) felt dislocated. When Gunde brought them back to the Middle East they were five, three and two. 'My younger daughter became completely Syrian – she started cursing America and all Zionists who had destroyed her country, just like all the other children in the camp were taught to do. She began to reject me in the street. She felt embarrassed because I was a foreigner. But I understood her need to do this, her need to create an identity for herself in this society.'

Gunde said that she had never missed Germany, although her daughters spoke fluent German and attended lectures and films at the Goethe Institut. She had always felt happy with the Palestinians and Syrians and had always been welcomed among them. 'I am a foreigner twice over as a German and as a Palestinian by marriage. But here Palestinians are entitled to everything that a Syrian is entitled to.' The most difficult time for her – as for all Westerners – had been during the Gulf War. Syria officially supported the Allies, but the vast majority of the people supported Saddam Hussein. 'All the Palestinians supported Iraq because of the terrible way the governments of the Gulf States had treated them, using them as cheap labour. They even tried to make demonstrations in Yarmuk on the streets but they were crushed.' The secret police were everywhere then. People attempted to receive Jordanian television, as Jordan was on the opposing side. Anyone seen on their roof trying to adjust their aerial was either beaten up or arrested. Anyone uttering opinions sympathetic to Iraq received the same treatment, including one thirteen-year-old girl who unwisely spoke out of turn in the school yard. She was thrown into prison.

We had by now arrived in Yarmuk, and in the darkness made our way past a sad-looking children's playground to Gunde's block. Inside we were greeted by one of her daughters, Leila, who had an olive complexion with dark blond hair and green eyes. It was a small flat but very clean, lined with books and pictures. In the sitting room were a few items from her husband's family home in Beit Safafa, near Bethlehem: an old pearl-studded chest, a heavy mahogany carved coffee grinder. On the wall was a tapestry, a naive and romanticized view of village life in Beit Safafa made in Gunde's workshop. 'This is the sort of thing we sell to rich Palestinians living in America as souvenirs of their homeland,' explained Gunde. 'It's what helps keep us afloat.

'At first we did nothing to make our home particularly comfortable,' she went on, 'because we thought we were just in the camp for a short while. People in Yarmuk are not owners, just builders. After six years we realized we were here for a long time, possibly for good, and tried to make it more of a home. Now in the camp people are worried what will happen to their homes if there is a peace pact. Will the government give them the land? Will they be able to buy it or to rent it?'

Inside, it did not feel as though we were in a refugee camp, or that the building probably did not have proper foundations or insulation. It was a little oasis detached from the immensely precarious and desperate life that was going on outside the front door. Gunde's young son had suffered from meningitis, and was now living with his father in Germany, where he was receiving special treatment. I asked Gunde why she did not take her daughters and return to Germany too. 'And abandon the workshop and all our projects? And all the women who depend on it?' she replied. 'I could not possibly do that for a minute.'

I left the apartment agreeing to meet Gunde at lunch-time the next day in the film festival office so we could pick up the programme, and took a taxi back to the town centre. I got out at Martyrs Square and bought a sandwich in a kebab shop. Jihad was sitting in the café again, talking to some Sudanese youths. I took my sandwich over. 'Look,' he said with a grin.

I saw a pale turquoise glass earring in his left ear. 'I like that,' I said. 'How did you do it?'

'After I saw you I bought it in the souk and put it in.'

'I hope you sterilized it,' I remarked mother-henishly.

'Yes. With olive oil. Where you go now?'

'Going to bed,' I said. 'Hotel.'

'No. You come with me now? Tea at my place?' His brown eyes looked up at me enquiringly. He was wearing a black vest with capped sleeves rolled up which emphasized the strong muscles in his upper arms. The words Yves Saint Laurent were embroidered on his shirt, which was so tight even his nipples were visible in outline through the fabric.

'No, not now,' I said. 'I can't. Maybe tomorrow.'

But I was intrigued to see how and where this strange man lived. I made a mental note to return to the café the next evening to see if he was there. An Arab with an earring in Syria is an Arab with chutzpah. Of that there could be no mistake.

Almost Untouched

Damascus, and specifically the Al Haramein, was the perfect place in which to kill time. I was enjoying myself immensely, so much so that I almost forgot that I was waiting for Rupert to return with my six hundred dollars. I fell in love with Sarouja. Often in the afternoon I would lie in my bed dozing, listening to the canaries that the shopkeepers kept imprisoned in small square cages hanging above their doors, trilling their hearts away into the vines that lay in a great web beneath my window. Just to stroll through these crumbling streets, poised as they were on the brink of destruction, was a poignant experience – watching this community struggling in the face of the redevelopment that encroached on it from all sides, robbing it week by week of all those characteristics that endowed the area with its own sense of history, tradition and identity.

In order to learn something more about Sarouja and its fate I contacted, through the British Council, Nadia Khoust, a famous campaigning journalist whom I had heard about in Aleppo. I had first seen her name in a large photographic book about the old houses of Syria, which I had found in a bookshop in Salhiya and which I could not resist buying. Inside was page upon page of detailed photographs of the grandest and oldest houses, with their elaborate stucco work and painted wall and ceiling decorations, their marble basins, courtyards, *liwans*, archways, pillars and fretwork balconies. Many of them, Khoust pointed out in her introduction, existed today only in these images. 'These antiquities deserve to be protected and saved,' she wrote, 'exactly as the Temple of Abu Simbul was protected from the water of the High Dam in Egypt.' Looking around Suk Sarouja, I feared that her words had been falling on deaf ears.

A former chairman of the Syrian Writers Union, Dr Khoust was a well-known media figure. At times she had been considered an extremist and to have acted high-handedly in this role, having expelled several fellow members of the Union for voicing their support for *Atatbiya* (normalization – referring to the realignment of cultural relations with Israel should peace finally be achieved). This was currently a sensitive issue in intellectual circles. Khoust was one of those who believed that there must never be normalization of cultural relations, even after conclusion of a peace pact. She and those who shared her view felt that there should only be economic and diplomatic ties between the two countries. 'I like Nadia very much,' a well-known playwright told me one day over coffee, 'but her actions led to the expulsion of the poet Adonis from the Writers Union, and I am against this. What is a writers' circle for if not to exchange ideas? For me the Writers Union should be a place of debate where we can express opposing views if we wish to. I cannot see it as a sort of party organization, although of course it is funded by the Party. As for Nadia's campaign to save Sarouja, I think she is fighting a losing battle and she should face it. But that is Nadia for you – she is the friend of lost causes.'

Nonetheless Khoust's stand on the preservation of architecture was a courageous one, and because she operated only in the cultural arena, she could get away with criticisms of government policy which would have incurred swift retaliation had she been operating in any more political sphere.

When I phoned her, she said she was free to meet me later that morning and would come to my hotel. 'I know it very well. It is a lovely place and Mr Dabbagh, the owner, is my friend.' When she arrived she was graciously received by Mr Dabbagh, who sent his youngest son out to buy some cakes. She was a woman in late middle age with blond, neatly bobbed hair and a pale, angular face. I had heard it said that her family was of Circassian origin. She was wearing a pale green two-piece suit and a blouse with a big bow, and could have been any well-dressed provincial English lady. She spoke quickly and animatedly in English, and had brought with her a copy of the book she had written about Sarouja specifically to raise public awareness of its fate. It featured numerous pictures of the area's decaying buildings, still beautiful but irrevocably damaged.

'The first thing to tell you,' she said, almost as soon as we had met, 'is that the street outside the door of your hotel is called Joset Al Hedba, which means "the nut tree of the hunchbacked woman".' I loved such quaint facts, and lapped them up. 'The second is that this whole area was built in the eleventh century by the Sitt Al Sham, which means the Lady of Damascus, who was none other than the sister of Saladin. Yes! The sister of Saladin!' she repeated, as if I had asked her to confirm it. 'That is what respect they are paying the history of this town. I grew up in this area. Our house was so beautiful with its lemon and orange trees, its courtyard and fountain. The traditional home, with its water, flowers, fruit trees and mosaics, was a little paradise shut away from the rest of the world, with its back to the busy, dangerous street. But now where is our old house?' (Dr Khoust displayed the Syrian habit of asking a question and then answering it on your behalf.) 'I will tell you where it is: *under the flyover!* That is how they operate here. They take the most beautiful parts first and destroy them so they can say to the public: Look, it's just a few old houses they are talking about. What's so special about these?'

Dr Khoust took me for a walk around the area, occasionally treading briskly in her clean court shoes over piles of rubble and builder's gravel. Clearly she refused to be defeated or dismayed in her eccentric passions, and instinctively I took a great liking to her.

'This area was the first extramural area to be built outside the walls of the old city,' she told me. 'It is very, very old. Most of the houses are two hundred years old, but they have been the site of continuous habitation since the beginning of the eleventh century.' As we walked up the Street of the Nut Tree of the Hunchbacked Woman, as I now knew to call it, she pointed out the inlaid flower pattern in the cobbled pavement. 'This is Ottoman. Most of them have been dug up or tarred over. Now the main axis is here – this is designed by Saladin's sister. As you can see, there is a Mameluke mosque, the Rose Mosque as it is called, and over there a little drinking fountain in the square which has stood there since the turn of the century. You had everything you needed in these streets, and everything in its proper place in relation to everything else. Now these modern developments are inhuman, everything scattered, inconvenient. There was also perspective. Can you see a beautiful minaret with a ball on it at the end of the street? Well, I saved that view. They wanted to block it out with a square modern building. How that would have ruined the sense of harmony, of perspective.'

Further down the street we found an ancient bath-house called the Hammam Al Joset. 'Now it is closed down, but it was built in the eleventh century and was functioning until a few years ago. The point about the bath-houses was that they were always built in the

Entrance to the Citadel at Aleppo.

Qalb Lozeh at Aleppo.

Courtyard of the Azem Palace at Damascus.

Salah-Eddin Citadel at Lattakia.

Damascus, neighbours look on as a lamb is slaughtered in honour of a pilgrim returned from Mecca. (Photograph by Ed Kashi.)

The image of President Hafez al-Assad appears everywhere, including the *suq* in the Old City of Dasmascus. (Photograph by Ed Kashi.)

The bazaar at Damascus.

A street scene in Damascus.

The market place of ancient Palmyra.

Part of the Theatre, with a section of the Grand Colonnade behind at Palmyra.

The Temple of Bel at Palmyra.

The amphitheatre at Bosra.

Jihad, a former commando in Lebanon.

A Syrian-held section of the Golan Heights, a family of Druze shout greetings to relatives in Israeli-occupied territory. (Photograph by Ed Kashi.)

centre of the residential area, so we know when this area was first inhabited from its date.'

She pointed to a map in her book. 'You see, this was Damascus in 1930. It basically then still comprised the old city. Now all this, all of it' – she indicated what had once been oasis – 'is suburbs. The gardens and orchards along the Barada River have gone, and the result is that even the climate now has changed. The city has become extremely hot, noisy and polluted. What have the developers done? I'll tell you what they've done: they've changed the climate! It is hell to live here in summer.'

To try to prevent as much destruction as possible, Dr Khoust had helped set up a commission. 'It was made entirely of academics and people from the university in order to avoid anyone with economic interests in the area getting on to it,' she explained. 'Now it is impossible to build in this area, but some of the developers are unfortunately also owners of the properties here and they are allowing the houses to fall down. Other owners have not restored their properties as they don't know what the future of this area will be. The construction that has been happening is following the 1936 plan of the French Mandate. They wanted to raze the whole of Suk Sarouja and redevelop it in the interests of "security, order and beauty", if you please! But they, they at least were French. Now it is the Syrians themselves who are destroying their history.'

All around us as we walked we could see beautiful houses askew, sagging and collapsing onto themselves like melting chocolate. The one at the end of the street where the hotel stood, near the little café, had a shop at the bottom, but the two storeys above were now reduced to mere wooden frames. The one next to that had collapsed altogether.

'Isn't it too late for this poor area now?' I dared to ask Nadia.

'No! Never! It is never too late,' she replied sharply. 'Now here, this is the shrine of Prince Soudon, which is called the Balamaniya. He was brought back to Damascus in chains by Tamburlaine, who killed him and then took his house. Further down here we have the Ayubbid shrines of Saladin's sister and brothers and her husband. You know they wanted to turn this courtyard where Saladin's sister lies buried into a carpark?'

As we passed the sad houses with their large shuttered casements overhanging the street, Dr Khoust showed me the delicate *mishrabi-yas* or latticed balconies, once used for keeping milk cool by means of the air currents that flowed through them. She knew all the houses like old friends: here lived a former cabinet minister, there a president, while over there was the house of some long-dead novelist or poet.

'Now these houses are considered very working-class. It is like the old city. Only the working class live there now. The middle classes have gone to the European-style suburbs.' Ironically this included Dr Khoust and her family, who lived in the fashionable (but dull) Mezze district. It was the only way a middle-class family could find the standard of living they required. This evacuation of the educated classes from the area had helped seal the fate of the old town houses.

But one house, the Beit Nizam, some way from Sarouja in the Christian quarter of the old city and formerly the British consulate, where Richard Burton had served as consul, was being painstakingly restored to create a small exclusive hotel, although it would not be open for a few more years. At least, Dr Khoust said, this was a step in the right direction. 'We endorse anything that gives these beautiful old buildings a relevant task in our contemporary cultural life, rather than just destroying them for the real-estate value of the land. The problem is that the government is not interested in financing "preservation". They just see it as a loss of money.'

The tomb of Saladin's sister was locked. Dr Khoust said she had an appointment but would phone me the next day to let me know when I could go and see it. 'It is well worth it. The roof and the walls are beautifully painted,' she said. 'Please, I hope you can write something about this. Every little may help to avert this terrible destruction.'

I returned to the hotel, where I too had an appointment, with a young Palestinian guide called Hussein Hinawi. I had been given his name and number by the writer Mary Lovell, who had recently completed a life of Jane Digby, the renegade nineteenth-century traveller who spent her last thirty years in Syria. I had first come across Jane Digby El Mezrab when I read Lesley Blanche's fascinating book *The Wilder Shores of Love*, about four different European women who found sexual or emotional fulfilment in the Middle East. Mary had suggested that Hussein might be able to take me to see Jane's house. If so I would be the first Westerner to visit it since its sale after her death.

Hussein, a Syrian-born Palestinian, was waiting for me. He en-

quired after his friend Mrs Lovell, and I answered his questions as
best I could. Then he said, 'I thought the best thing would be first of
all to find the grave of Madame Digby. Then to go and visit her
house, which is in the Har Al Aksab, some four kilometres away from
the centre.'

We took a taxi in the direction of the airport and headed for the
Protestant cemetery. It was rush hour and we had plenty of time to
talk in the cab. 'You are familiar with the life of Madame Digby, I
presume?' asked Hussein. I replied that I knew the basic facts – that
she spent a lot of her childhood playing in the grounds of Holkham
Hall, her grandfather Lord Leicester's Palladian villa designed by
Inigo Jones, and from these privileged beginnings had gone on to
marry, too young, a respectable but dull peer, Lord Ellenborough,
who was later Viceroy of India. She never became his consort,
however, because her very public affair with a Prince Felix Schwarzenberg became the great scandal of Regency London. (A curious
fact that had lodged in my journalist's mind was that public interest
in the affair was so high that *The Times*, which ordinarily carried
only classified adverts on its front page, dropped them for the first
time in its history in order to lead on Jane Digby's divorce. I have
always borne this fact in mind when people who read *The Times* tell
me sniffily that they would never allow a tabloid into the house.)

Thereafter Lady Ellenborough fled in disgrace to the Continent,
bore two children to Schwarzenberg, who dumped her, was outcast
by French society, and moved on to Germany. In Munich she had an
affair with King Ludwig I of Bavaria, giving birth to his daughter,
who later died in a lunatic asylum. She then married a kind baron,
Theotoky, who adored her, but abandoned him for a young Greek
nobleman and thus acquired a taste for dark moustaches that led to
her fulfilment in the most unlikely of circumstances.

'So you know why it was she was destined to come to Syria?'
Hussein asked me. I said I would appreciate it if he could expand my
limited knowledge.

'She was in love with a wild man whom she met in Athens. And
she came to Syria to buy him a pure-bred Arab stallion. Lady Digby
was a fine horsewoman. Her lover was called General Xristodolos
Hadji Petros – a warlord like those we still have in this part of the
world, such as Walid Junblatt, the warlord of the Druze mountains
in Lebanon. Petros led a band of Albanian mercenaries called the
Pallikares which the King enlisted to defend Athens. He was thought

to be the lover of Queen Amalie of Athens – who was married to a nephew, I think, of King Ludwig, who was Lady Digby's lover.'

As we churned through the traffic we could see electric oriental crosses lit up in the dusk, indicating that we were approaching the cemetery. Many of the tombs were decorated with these devices.

I reflected that Jane Digby was one of the first Western outcasts to find acceptance and fulfilment in the Middle East. What was the enigma that drew the lonely and detached – Burton, Lawrence, Lady Hesther Stanhope, Jane Digby, Gertrude Bell, Wilfred Thesiger – to a community that has such strong rules, such cohesion and ultimately such conformism? Perhaps it was the warmth, hospitality and security of that community which appealed to strangers, allied with the special allowance made for the outsider, who would never perhaps be expected to conform in the same way as its own members. Being a foreigner in an alien culture is a way of institutionalizing your aloneness, of going public with it. You are no longer failing to meet the expectations and values of your own world, nor do you have to meet those of your adopted one – or if you do, no one expects you to do it perfectly.

'A terrible thing happened to her,' Hussein went on. 'When she was married to the Count Theotoky she gave birth to one son whom she adored as her own life. He was her darling Leonidas. And it was of this child that she carried a miniature in her luggage for the rest of her life. Unlike her other children, she took this child away from his father when she left him, but then something really dreadful happened.'

'What was that?'

'After leaving Theotoky in Corfu, she went to Lucca in Italy and hired a beautiful villa. It had an open hall which was forty feet high and a staircase that wound round and round to the top floor. Well, one day little Leonidas was alone in the top of this house and he saw his mother downstairs in the hall. He so loved his mother he wanted to show off to her, and he tried to slide down the banisters to get her attention and praise. But he flew off the banisters and crashed down by her feet, dying before her very eyes. After this Madame Digby almost lost the will to live, just wandering without a purpose, travelling around Egypt and falling ill with malaria, which occurred for the rest of her life. Only when she came to Syria to buy her lover, the general, a pure Arab stallion did she find the peace she was seeking.'

'How was that?'

'She met here her great and last love, an Arab sheikh.'

I remembered this part – how she had been guided across the desert to Palmyra by Sheikh Medjuel et Mezrabi, whose family had been appointed by the Ottomans to lead people of distinction across the sands, and how she had married him and lived in Damascus for half the year, spending the other half following the migrations in the desert, living in Bedouin tents and using all the skills she had learned at Holkham Hall to train horses and breed sheep and even camels, as if running a mobile estate.

'You know she even rode into battle with her husband?' asked Hussein. 'You must know about the Ghazzou?'

'Well, only a little,' I admitted.

'The Ghazzou is a ritual battle that takes place among the Bedouin tribesmen. It is very ancient and your Crusaders used it as the basis for the medieval jousts they held to honour their ladies. You see, there are very specific rules to the Ghazzou. People are rarely killed. Often, though, they are injured, or even taken as captives. Madame Digby fought alongside her husband, and by this time she was in her fifties and wearing Arab dress, with a long plait of hair and kohl all around the edge of her blue eyes. And all the tribesmen and women loved her, calling her Umm Al Laban, Mother of Milk, after her white, white skin.'

In Damascus Jane Digby led a more sedate life, wearing out-of-date European clothes. She had a wide circle of friends, including the Algerian Emir Abd El Kader, then languishing in exile after his revolt against the French, Colonel Charles Churchill, Druze historian, and the explorer and Arabist Richard Burton and his wife Isabel. Burton, like Jane, was a great linguist and student of native culture, and would discuss with her her extensive knowledge of harem life – the one area of Arab society he was not able to penetrate with his flawless Arabic, dark looks, and love of native dress.

Later in life Jane befriended the Blunts. Wilfred Scawen Blunt was a writer whose wife, Lady Anne, was Byron's only granddaughter, and they came to Syria on various occasions to buy breeding stock from the oldest Arab bloodlines in order to set up the first Arabian stud, the Crabbet Stud, in England in 1878. Medjuel was a great authority on the bloodlines, and imparted much valuable information to the couple. 'Mrs Digby has the traces of great beauty and now, even with the most unfavourable style of dress [Jane often resorted to native garb], she appears a person of distinction,' wrote Lady Anne. 'Her manner is perfectly quiet, dignified and unassuming.'

Medjuel was the final and most permanent addition to her exotic *galère* of lovers. He was small, graceful and very dark – so dark as to make Isabel Burton write in 1896, 'The contact with that black skin, I could not understand. Her Sheikh was very dark, darker than a Persian and much darker than an Arab generally is. All the same he was a very intelligent and charming man in any light but as a husband. That made me shudder.' However, Jane found almost perfect happiness with this man, who, unlike so many others (Theotoky and Hadji Petros, to name but two), never showed any interest in her considerable personal wealth. After his death the money she had left him was found tied up in packets under his bed. It had been kept purely as a souvenir of her, almost untouched.

Jane Digby became a *cause célèbre*, and was also visited by the Prince of Wales, the Emperor of Brazil and Barty Mitford – later to become Lord Redesdale and the father of the famous Mitford sisters – who left this sketch: 'I found Lady Ellenborough – Mrs Digby, as she now calls herself – living in a European house, furnished so far as the rooms in which we were received were concerned like those of an English lady. In the desert with her tribe she would be altogether Arab.' It was this house that I was hoping to visit later.

The Protestant cemetery where Jane Digby is buried is an orderly Victorian cemetery. Her grave is surrounded by those of the people she would have known well in the Damascus of the late nineteenth century. The gravestone, when we located it, was quite a simple, understated affair, standing beneath a tree with a large cross on top. Along the side could be read the words: 'Jane Elizabeth, daughter of Admiral Sir Henry Digby GCB. Born April 3rd 1807. Died Aug. 11th 1881.' Engraved below was a line from the Psalms: 'My trust is in the tender mercy of God for ever and ever.' It appeared to be an entirely conventional tombstone, bereft of any references to her four marriages, five children, her defiantly unconventional life, her pursuit of love and happiness beyond the security of all else – often that of her own children – or her life of sexual exile. Entirely conventional save for one thing: a slab of pink limestone from Palmyra placed at the end of the grave on which, carved in Arabic by the husband who finally brought her happiness and fulfilment and who held his exotic wife in such high regard, were the simple words:

'Madame Digby El Mezrab'. It was Medjuel's direct but affirmative last testament to their love.

We repaired to the taxi which plunged us into the spiralling series of ring roads enclosing modern Damascus. Eventually, both feeling totally disoriented, we arrived at Har Al Aksab, which appeared to be a completely drab and commonplace suburb. Hussein had only visited it once previously himself, and he had to keep a sharp eye out for familiar landmarks. We paid off the driver and walked in the direction of a very old mosque. Next to it was a modern block which Hussein explained had been built in the grounds of Jane Digby's house. 'You see, the property has been divided up, and there are at least thirty families now living on the site. All of them are very poor. There are, however, one or two original rooms.'

I longed to go into the garden to see where Mrs Digby had kept her ménage of animals. She was said to have kept over a hundred cats, various horses and dogs, and even a pelican.

Running beneath the mosque was an unlit corridor entered from the street through an entirely nondescript archway. We followed this dark tunnel until we reached its end. To the left there was another passageway into what, in the gathering darkness, looked like a fragment of courtyard; to the right stood two doors. Hussein knocked on the one in front of us and we heard shuffling inside. 'It is a very old poor man who lives here now,' Hussein whispered to me. 'I hope you do not mind, but I think it most convenient if I introduce you as Lady Digby's descendant.' I replied that I did not mind in the least, mentally making my apologies to Mrs Digby.

The door opened to reveal a stooping, slovenly-looking man in his late sixties, dirty, unshaven and wearing thick-lensed black glasses. He duly conducted us into his little den and gestured towards the bed, which was uninvitingly covered by a knot of none-too-clean rags. We perched on the edge of the mattress. The bed stood in the corner of the room, and on each wall was a decayed ornate niche decorated with the carved wooden mouldings Jane Digby had designed herself. On the walls was some rather faded pale blue wallpaper in a foliate design, clearly dating from the construction of the house and probably imported from Paris.

The old man sat on a little stool by a table illuminated by a wavering, watery beam from a naked bulb which hung from a frayed piece of cable attached to the ceiling by a series of pins. He started to roll himself a cigarette. On the floor at his feet was a tray of lentils soaking in water. He had two cats which looked faintly put out by the arrival of visitors. I was sure Mrs Digby would have approved of them. He stood and bustled about, making tea and talking to the floor. He said that his grandfather had known the Signora – as he called her – and had bought the house from her son (by whom he meant, in fact, her stepson). The Mezrabis had now gone to live in Saudia Arabia. They were Bedouins, not town people. The old man had inherited this sliver of the house, which had once been one of its crowning glories. I was allowed to prowl around and look at the fireplace, which had been painted over. As I did so I experienced the creepy sensation of a myriad of cobwebs wrapping themselves around my head. I was considerably taller than the present stunted incumbent, and my head was able to graze those spidery recesses his bowed one never would.

The room in which we sat – despite its filth and untidiness – had clearly once been beautiful. It was an odd shape – square with an octagonal domed roof. The old man had constructed a rickety staircase and a false ceiling to make this dome into a second room. He took us upstairs, and I noticed a beautiful ceiling rose still in place with golden mouldings of leaves and fruit and little pieces of mirror-work set into it, matching those surviving on the cupboard doors below. High in the dome were little windows.

'If we could have access to the roof,' Hussein said, 'we would be able to look over the rooftops of Damascus as Jane did during the massacre of the Christians by the Druze and the Ottomans in 1860. It was a horrific time, and she witnessed crowds of women, some carrying children, fleeing across the flat roofs of the Christian quarter, which traditionally is how all our women moved about the city, in privacy. Some of them, however, plunged headlong into the flames.'

Hussein told me that about two thousand people had been slaughtered in three days (sixteen thousand in the country as a whole), including some European missionaries and teachers. Mrs Digby and her husband gave sanctuary to as many Christians as could make it to the very house we were now standing in, while its gates were guarded by Bedouin tribesmen. The bitterness between Druze and Christians had been simmering for some time, and had been exacerbated by the anti-Christian Ottoman authorities. After the riots, Jane bravely went about the city in native dress to inspect the damage and try to help those families she knew to be boarded up in their houses.

The whole experience was a trauma for her, and led to her taking Communion in the Anglican church for the first time in thirty-six years.

I went back down the rickety staircase. 'Does the owner know that the future King of England came here once, and that the Emperor of Brazil and other great personages of the period were guests?' I asked Hussein. He translated my words for the old man. The concept of the King of England visiting his humble dwelling was clearly as inconceivable to him as the prospect of Haroun Al Rashid turning up at my house on a milk float was to me. He looked blank, shaking his head and mumbling something. 'He says,' Hussein translated back, 'that he only knows what he has told us, and also that Jane Digby called herself the Signora because relations were very bad with the Ottoman authorities of the time and she wanted to disguise her English background.'

This certainly seemed to fit in with the story of the massacre. I later read in Mary Lovell's book how Jane had become outraged to learn that as a result of marrying an Ottoman subject she forfeited her British nationality and technically became a Turk.

We lingered in the house, drinking sweet sticky tea out of dirty glasses, more to keep the old man company than anything else. Hussein chatted respectfully to him in the way the Arab young do to the elders of their community, regardless of class or profession, and after a while we left. Hussein had to hurry back to meet a tourist group, for whom I had no doubt he would provide a service as efficient and conscientious as the one he had provided for me. I thanked him for his help and he gave me four cards – gold-edged on pearly paper. There was a picture of some Roman ruins embossed in gold in the top left-hand corner. I was always intrigued by the sheer fussiness of the personal cards I was handed in Syria, often printed by the oldest letterpress machines you could imagine. Even the embassy and the British Council staff presented you with them. I thanked Hussein for his help and kindness and offered him some money. He would not accept it, saying: 'The only thing you can do for me is recommend my services as a guide to anyone coming to Syria from England.' Which I hope, in some small measure, I have done.

16

Jihad?

That evening I went to the café in Martyrs Square, more than half hoping that I would find Jihad. He was sitting there talking to a group of shifty-looking North Africans. He was wearing a faded denim shirt, unbuttoned down to his navel, making visible a smooth olive chest with a dramatic gash across it. 'Hello. How's the earring?' I asked. He turned his head and I could see that the area surrounding it was red and becoming infected. 'You must get some disinfectant,' I explained, but he looked uncomprehending.

We left the café. He was determined that I should visit his house, and by dint of not refusing I had consented to go with him. Darkness was falling, the soft light making everything seem even older and more mysterious than it already was. Jihad's house was near the now nearly empty Jewish area, Haret-Yehud, and he led me on a wonderfully serpentine route through alleyways, under archways, behind the Great Mosque and past the less well-preserved remains of the Roman gateway at the rear. I realized that this was a route that people had taken for hundreds of years. If you came to a flyover or a dual carriageway you simply walked under or over it and carried on regardless.

I was always intrigued at this time of evening by the barbers' shops – little islands of Victorian anachronism, with cloaked customers enthroned in great silver chairs, heads tilted back, being shaved with a cut-throat razor before vast, speckled Belle Epoque mirrors.

As we were walking it struck me rather belatedly that I ought to have found out more about Jihad before I went back to his house. I was, after all, carrying over a thousand dollars in cash in the little canvas money belt secreted beneath my shirt, which might prove too great a temptation to resist in a society where the average wage was fifteen dollars a week. I asked Jihad if he lived with his family, as I had presumed. 'No, I never talk to my father or my mother. They live near by and send food to me. But they think I am crazy,' he replied. This was hardly reassuring. I seemed to remember from various newspaper articles I had read in recent years that one of the signs of the serial killer is that he lives alone and has no bonds with any members of his family or the community. What if Jihad knocked me out cold when we got back to his place? It was pitch black now, and I had no idea where we were. I must be off my trolley, I thought in mounting panic. This man is clearly a nut, a loner, an outsider. But of course, that was precisely why I had agreed to go with him. The whole evening was overlaid with the familiar excitement that risk never fails to induce.

We eventually plunged into a dark alleyway. I looked over my shoulder. No one had seen us. If anything happened to me now I was a goner: Jihad was much more powerful than me. We crossed an ancient courtyard with uneven flags on the floor, heading for the far corner. Before us was a battered old doorway with most of the paint peeling off. Jihad took out his keys and undid the padlock and chain. The door was off its hinges, and he grasped it firmly, picked it up and deposited it to the side, as if he were King Kong. 'Come,' he said gruffly, and took hold of my hand. I followed. There was a mad scrabbling noise and a skeletal cat jumped onto the window ledge and squirmed through a little hole in the frame. 'Ah, Beebee, Beebee,' Jihad called.

'Who's Beebee?' I asked, as much for the sake of making conversation as anything else.

'My cat,' said Jihad. If a man is nice to a cat he can't be all bad, I reasoned desperately. He switched on the light. The room was a dark, poverty-stricken hovel with dirty pale blue walls and a black ceiling where the chimney from the stove in the middle petered out and had belched out its fumes. There was a rickety metal-framed bed with a table beside it. Above the bed was a built-in cupboard, full of pots and pans. On the door and the wall above the bed, as on a GI's locker, were pasted pictures of mouth-watering young girls, cut out from magazines. At the foot of the bed, covered in dark brown army blankets, was a dilapidated couch. In a far corner there was a pile of rags and old newspapers. This, it would appear, was Jihad's home.

'Do you live here alone?' I asked him, not quite knowing what I wanted the answer to be. In any event, he replied simply, 'Sometimes.' He gestured for me to sit down, which I did, and disappeared from the room carrying a tray of glasses and a teapot. The only

source of water appeared to be the tap in the loo in the courtyard
outside.

Jihad returned and, pulling a selection of live wires from a socket
and substituting them for some others, connected up an electric ring
onto which he placed a tin kettle. He sat near by on the bed, and
when the kettle had boiled I noticed that he lifted his feet up before
handling the kettle.

'Why do you lift your feet up like that, Jihad?' I asked him.

'Electricity,' he said. 'From here to here to here.' He pointed from
the metal bedstead to the metal bedside table to the electric ring to
the tin kettle and finally to his heart. 'If I wear shoes with *zeldj* ...
What is *zeldj* in English?'

'Leather.'

'OK, leather. If I wear with leather, no problem. If I don't I get ...
what do you say in English?'

'You get a shock.'

'*Tamanan*. A shock.'

'Could it kill you?'

He pulled a long maybe-yes-maybe-no sort of face. 'Who cares?'
he said, with his odd, slightly mad smile.

He reached for his packet of evil Hamara cigarettes and offered
me one.

'No, look, let me buy you some,' I said. 'I need some myself. I
can't smoke those. I have to have a special sort with mint. You know,
menthol.'

I knew that according to Arab etiquette I would not be allowed to
buy anything myself as a guest. He would have to go to the shop, and
I suddenly thought that I could go with him and see how he was
greeted. If he did turn out to be the mad axeman at least there would
be witnesses to my visit. At the same time I felt guilty, for I instinctively trusted and liked him.

'We go after tea,' said Jihad, handing me a glass.

He sat down next to me. His presence was comforting rather than
threatening, so close that I could see the scar on his pectoral muscle.
'Jihad, what is that?' I couldn't resist asking.

'What?'

'That scar.'

'What is scar?' he asked.

'Look, here.' I touched the fine line which was intersected with
little crosses where the stitches had once been, wondering if he

would slug me in the mouth as an Englishman would probably have done.

'From the commandos.'

'What commandos?'

'All of us. We are all commandos. Aged sixteen, seventeen, eighteen. A long time ago. We were in Lebanon, fighting Israelis.' Half a lifetime ago (he was now thirty-three, I later learned).

He undid the rest of his shirt and pulled it open so that I could see the full extent of the scar. Then he shrugged the shirt off. He had a smooth olive torso, now a little out of condition but with large groups of muscles: a broad sweep of pectorals crowned with fleshy, square-tipped nipples, a long, narrow stomach, broad and meaty shoulders. His arms were strong and sinewy. When he pointed at his chest I could see a powerful bicep moving beneath the glossy skin.

'Here too.' He pointed to two small scars in the middle of his sternum. These he said were knife wounds. 'And here.' He twisted round so that his back was facing me. 'More scars.' His back had two weals across it. 'And here.' He took my fingers and placed them under his wavy hair at the base of his skull where it joined the neck. There was a hard lump where some shrapnel had lodged and had never been removed. He was a beaten-up old thing, like a battle-torn but friendly old tomcat. I suddenly reflected that I had got myself into a very intimate position with this man, but I felt perfectly comfortable and relaxed. I would never have believed that an ex-Palestinian terrorist could be so gentle and sweet-natured.

He lifted up my glass of tea and offered it to me, then put his arm around me. He looked so vigorous and attractive, yet his life had to some extent petered out. What was he doing trapped in this dead end in life? And here was I, a voyeur, a tourist.

'Come on,' I said, 'let's go to the shop.'

He put on his small black vest and guided me to the door. In the street he linked arms with me and we strolled along contentedly. I thought, Why do I never feel like this with English people? But the Middle East is a great place for misfits, people who cannot relate to their own kind.

There was a little square near by. We went into the shop and, to my relief, Jihad was greeted as a regular. I bought a couple of packets of Marlboro and some chocolates, then we wandered down to the ruined Roman arch and ordered sandwiches and juice in a bar. As we stood eating, a young man came in. His eye fell on Jihad's blue earring. A look of incredulity and disapproval, if not horror, suffused his face. Jihad noticed and looked at me, raising his eyes briefly to the ceiling, but continuing coolly to eat his sandwich. I wondered what made him want to draw attention to himself and set himself apart from the conventions of Syrian society. It showed a degree of self-confidence and independent thought that the average Arab would find threatening. Fortunately he was too powerfully built for anyone to tangle with him. And it was precisely this combination which the man in the bar could not deal with. Here was an obviously tough, macho guy, with an earring. It did not make sense.

'Are there many Jews in this area still?' I asked as we wandered back through the dark alleyways.

'Many of them left a few years ago. Now all their houses are empty. This one Jewish house – and this one. All empty now. All gone. And here, this is church for Jews.' He jerked his head at a building across the alleyway. It had chicken wire over the windows and looked neglected. I reflected that it was strange that Syrian Jews and Palestinians, both in a sense outcasts, should live side by side in this poor area. Jihad's own family had come from Akko, now part of Israel, and he was living right next to the Jewish area. 'What do you think of the Jews?' I asked him.

'They are very nice people. We get on well with them,' he replied simply, and to my surprise. I had been expecting a tirade. Until the mid-fifties there were communities of Jews living successfully all over the Middle East, but the founding of Israel had put an end to that. Many times in Syria people, young and old, would say to me, shaking their heads, 'Ah, Robert. Why? Why did you do it?', referring, I assumed, to the governments of the Western powers, but making it sound as though it was I who was personally responsible for the establishment of the Israeli state. Their tone implied: 'You seem such a nice person. How *could* your government have done this to us?' Jihad, though, was different. He never asked why the world had turned out this way. He just chuckled dryly, not wanting explanations, or involvement. He got on with mending his watches.

We were back near Jihad's house. He told me that there was a shop near my hotel that was run by the leader of the Jewish community. The owner, Mr Jayati, employed a Palestinian assistant. I found this notion very strange, and cynically wondered if the shop-owner did so to enhance his credibility. But then why should we assume that all Jews have the same political thoughts? Many

Armenians who were pro-Western, like Baby Shoes, were strongly anti-American. Some Jews were presumably sympathetic to the Palestinian situation. In Syria the Jews had been heavily oppressed until fairly recently. They understood the nature of dispossession and discrimination if anyone did.

Jihad twiddled the dial on his radio. A warm gush of classical music swept over the room. 'Ah, Dvorak,' he sighed, and lay back on his bed like a connoisseur. As the music ebbed away, a male announcer with a chocolatey voice gabbled in soft Arabic and Chopin came over the airwaves. It was getting late.

'Jihad, thank you for tea. I must go now,' I said.

'Go? Where? Where are you going? Stay here with me.'

'That's very kind, but I think I should go back to the hotel.'

'Why hotel? Hotel is stupid. Stay here with me.'

'What do you mean? Where?' I said hopelessly, casting my eyes around the room.

'Here!' He banged the bed. 'Sleep here with me. Please. Don't go now.' He looked at me soulfully with beseeching brown eyes, making me feel mean and unreasonable.

Suddenly we were plunged into darkness. The Chopin stopped. It was a power cut. I felt Jihad very close by. He whispered into my ear: 'You see, *habibi. Maktub.*' It was written.

I found it difficult to sleep that night for a variety of reasons. I was mortally terrified that Jihad had put the live wires in the wrong hole and that when the electricity was reconnected we would be fried to death in the electric bed. Jihad was sleeping like a baby, one heavy arm encircling me, so I could not escape. I imagined the newspaper reports in London. It was just the sort of poetic justice that would serve me bloody well right, I thought grimly.

The second and equally chilling factor was that I was afraid the secret police would appear at any moment. Someone somewhere was bound to have seen me arrive, I reasoned. There couldn't be many *ajnabees* wandering through Haret-Yehud at this time of night. What on earth was I going to tell them? Was it going to get Jihad into trouble? He was Palestinian, and a potential political embarrassment. I might be perceived as a spy, running messages, arms, spreading discontent, whipping up grievances. Encouraging independent thought.

Eventually I did sleep. When I awoke, Jihad was wrapped around me, clutching me desperately as if he were drowning. All Middle Eastern men share beds with their best friends. In the great cult of male friendship, sleeping with someone is to demonstrate the level of your intimacy. Were it not for the reasons enumerated, I might have enjoyed the experience more. In the end I disentangled myself and stole out into the dawn, feeling guilty and furtive like a naughty schoolboy. I crossed the courtyard and slipped out into the passageway, and then into the street, pulling my cap down, rather futilely, over my eyes. I was sure that no one saw me leave.

17

Where Elijah Anointed Elisha

That morning I had arranged to attend an opera rehearsal at the Institute of Dramatic and Performing Arts, the school attached to the opera house. But first I wanted to go and see the Jewish shop-owner, Mr Jayati, and ask him for directions to an old synagogue on the outskirts of Damascus which the young diplomat had told me about. It was said to very beautiful but difficult to find.

Mr Jayati's shop was called Le grand magasin, and was a large men's clothing boutique. I wandered around the racks of dismal dark green and brown acrylic trousers and awful dark blue car coats. It was quite clear that there was nothing here I could possibly buy, not even for my father. On one wall was a framed photograph of Mr Jayati and the President, shaking hands. It was like a good-luck charm, a display of presidential approval. Even the churches displayed pictures of whoever their patriarch might be with the President. Unlike the Jews, however, the Christians had every reason to be grateful to Assad. The Jews had to smarm up to him whatever the circumstances (and they had fluctuated wildly in the last twenty years) and hope for the best.

Eventually an assistant approached me and asked if I required any help. I said I was wondering if it would be possible to see Mr Jayati. The assistant replied that Mr Jayati was not present but that his son, Murad, could help me. I was taken to a thin young man with dark hair and eyes and pale skin, wearing a tooth brace. He had a little gold trinket representing the Hebrew sign for God attached to his belt. Above him there was a photograph of him meeting President Clinton at the White House – he had gone one better than his father. He spoke good English.

'My father is not here. He left for New York this morning. But I

can take you to the synagogue if you wish. Now I must ask if you are
a tourist, or do you wish to see the synagogue for other reasons?'
    I replied that I was a tourist, and asked why he wanted to know.
    'Because first, if you are connected with the Western media, your
visit must be cleared with the Ministry of Information.'
    I clearly could not resort to this procedure as it would blow my
cover, which for a variety of reasons I did not wish to do. I therefore
maintained the lie that I was a tourist. We made an arrangement to
meet at two o'clock that afternoon.

The Institute of Dramatic and Performing Arts had been established
a few years previously, and its first graduations were due to take
place that year. It stood in glamorous Umawiya Square, near Abu
Romani, the embassy area, along with the headquarters of the Syrian
Broadcasting Company, the Sheraton Hotel and the Assad Library,
which had a large statue of the seated President outside it.
    From the outside the theatre presented a daunting prospect, with
large expanses of pale brown stone walls and a monumental gateway.
Inside it was vast, with a large presidential box bang in the middle of
the dress circle. There were also two smaller theatres. The school was
an extremely luxurious, spacious affair, alive with piano music
coming from the rehearsal rooms. I found Caroline in mid-rehearsal
in one of the studios. The sorceress was participating in a duet,
wrapped in her veil. 'It's such a pity. She has a fantastic voice but
psychologically and physically the presence of the veil is preventing
her from producing it,' said Caroline afterwards.
    The Institute was adorned with photographs of various produc-
tions and pictures of the great Russian playwrights, their names in
Cyrillic script, presumably remnants of the time when the Soviets
dominated Syria's cultural life. Caroline showed me around and
introduced me to the set designer, Numan Joud. I asked him if the
story of Dido and Aeneas was familiar to the Syrians. He said it was
not. Everyone had heard of Antony and Cleopatra, who had once
figured large in this part of the world (in fact Syria was part of
Cleopatra's wedding present), but no one knew anything about
Dido. It struck me that it would be a good idea to incorporate the
services of a *hakawati* or story-teller, such as I had seen reciting in
the café behind the Great Mosque. He could appear at the beginning
to relate the story so far in Arabic, a suggestion that Caroline happily
took up.

Later Numan took me to see the model of the set, and I noticed that it was dominated by a large sinister eye. 'That is the fate that always follows us,' he said mournfully. 'The fate over which we have no control. The Evil Eye.' For poor, doomed Dido, no symbol could have been more fitting.

I walked back along the road from Umawiya Square, following the course of the Barada River. It had been canalized and was full of litter. At a point almost opposite the museum, I cut through a small park, past the old school overlooking the main road, and found myself near the Peasants' Monument, which ironically stood on the roundabout in front of the five-star Cham Palace Hotel. To my left the road led to Salhiya, a smart middle-class area built in the nineteenth century where the Burtons had lived when they served at the consulate, before Richard was summarily dismissed for his pro-Arab views. Beyond Salhiya were the slopes of Mount Kassioun, up which the city had gradually crept in a rising tidal wave of conurbation, so that at night the whole mountainside was a bank of twinkling lights. There was an area of the mountain known as Foot, where Mohammad had stood to look over the ancient city beneath him which, with its gardens, orchards and rivers, he declared so beautiful as to rival paradise. He declined to enter it, deeming one paradise alone to be enough for him – the paradise of heaven rather than of man.

Damascus was far from a paradise today, even for the crabby old Aloui mountain goats who stood on its peaks. Most of it was not even beautiful any more, although it had a festering splendour which turned up unexpectedly here and there – in an exquisite tenth-century fountain choked with garbage, an ancient funerary college in magpie stone with domes and minarets, its walls plastered with peeling bills, the wonderful khans whose stately domes had collapsed in upon themselves and which now looked like eggshells gaping to the skies, but which were nevertheless bustling with porters, hawkers and merchants.

Hanging almost tangibly above all this was the feeling that the city was not really a happy place. There was always the dead albatross of suspicion and paranoia hanging around its neck. Perhaps its history of intolerance towards Christians was part of it. But it was also something to do with the oppressive nature of the system under whose yoke the town was grinding along (as four hundred years previously it had ground along under the somewhat more benign authoritarian rule of the Ottomans).

I made my way from the roundabout to Le grand magasin. Murad was locking up the shop, pulling down the aluminium shutters with an ear-splitting screech and securing them with padlocks. (The screeching of shutters is a sound I always associate with Syria. Countless times I was wakened from a blissful afternoon siesta or a deep night's sleep by this terrible jarring noise.) He led me to his car – a Peugeot, about ten years old, relatively new by Syrian standards.

The traffic was dense, giving us plenty of time to talk. Murad told me that we were going to the suburb of Jobar, which was about seven kilometres away. At one time, he said, there had been about twenty-two synagogues in Damascus. Most of them were closed now. This was the oldest, and was where Elisha was baptised by Elijah, although he believed there was an older one in Aleppo which dated from the time of King Solomon. This, I suspected, was the crumbling wreck behind Khandak which I had been warned by Baby Shoes not to investigate.

The Jewish community in Syria was one of the last in the Middle East to be forcibly held in a country against its wishes, as a useful pawn in the battle with Israel. The recent moves towards peace, and the realignment in the international pecking order since the collapse of the Soviet empire, meant that the fate of the Jewish community had become a useful lever in American bargaining power. 'Only a few years ago,' Murad explained, 'there were about two thousand Jews in Damascus with about three hundred in Qamishleh and seven hundred in Aleppo. Now there are under two hundred in Damascus, fifteen people in Aleppo and only one family in Qamishleh. Since Rabbi Hamra left Damascus in 1993 my father became the leader of the community. He's not a rabbi but a businessman. He keeps an eye on the synagogue and the cemetery.'

'How many of your family have left?' I asked.

'My first brother left in 1993 and then my other brother in 1994. They went to New York. There is a very large community of Syrian Jews there – about thirty thousand. But that only accounts for about twenty to thirty per cent of our community. The rest are scattered in Brazil, Argentina, Europe and Israel. I had three uncles who went to Israel in 1949. Many Jews left Syria at that time. A lot went illegally by boat from Beirut. The exodus was really 1946 to 1949. Before that time the Jewish community was very powerful in Damascus. Forty years ago we represented five per cent of the community.

'Post-1948, of course, things got very bad for us here. They stayed bad until 1992. That was the first big change for us. Things are so much better now. There is only one Jewish school left and it is forbidden to teach Hebrew – only the prayer service is taught and enough to read the Torah. I cannot speak Hebrew. Most of us speak in Arabic. It is our mother tongue.

'The seventies were the worst of all. From 1948 until 1977 no Jew was allowed to travel out of Damascus further than five kilometres. There were problems about owning property, which only became easier after 1992. Now everything is much better. I am staying here because somebody must run the family business. I do not have many friends any more and of course it is very difficult now to find a suitable girl to marry. There is hardly any choice.'

I asked him about relations with the Palestinians.

'It was always normal for us to have Islamic and Christian friends,' he said. 'We employ Christians in the shops and one Palestinian. We have good relations with them. We have agreed to live together. We live in an Arabic house in Haret-Yehud and we have Palestinian people living near us.'

I could not resist asking his opinion of the Israeli occupation of the West Bank.

'This is a political question and we are forbidden to discuss political matters, as you know. But between you and me, since you ask me that question, I do not think the occupation can be justified. I don't think what they have done can be right.'

I wondered whether this was really Murad's opinion, or whether he was one of the 'bourgeois negatives' cleared by the authorities to represent the community's 'views'. I concluded that you did not have to live in a free democracy to identify injustice when you saw it. One awful consequence of the police state is that you tend not to credit people with the integrity that is their due.

The car had swung down a side street pitted with potholes. Murad pulled up and we got out, making our way to an anonymous, low, brown building. There was no indication that it was a synagogue. Murad rang the bell and a little old man with no teeth appeared and conducted us into a courtyard with modern paving. In front of us was a pair of splendid beaten copper doors, richly engraved with the Menorah and other Jewish symbols. According to the date in Arabic above them, they had been made as recently as 1985. We took off our shoes and Murad and the concierge put on the yarmulke. They swung open an inner door to reveal a riot of carpets, lanterns, chandeliers and framed inscriptions. While many of the lamps were old and encrusted with a patina of dust and age, others looked as if they had come directly out of a Golders Green lighting emporium – Aladdin's lamps, some like glass vases embellished with gold arabesques, large brass domes from which hung smaller lamps fringed with beaded multicoloured curtains. In the middle of this cluttered room was a large octagonal pulpit, alongside which was an ancient Damascan settle inlaid with lemonwood, bone and mother of pearl.

According to Murad, who I suspected did not know very much about it, the synagogue dated from the sixth century, but had last been restored eighty years ago. A large marble tablet on the floor commemorated the place where Elisha had been anointed by Elijah. The concierge guided us to the far end of the room to two pairs of locked wooden doors set into two marble arches, behind which the Torah was kept. Chiselled all over the doors and the marble steps of this holiest of holies, like graffiti, were the names of the faithful of past decades. They were crudely executed in Arabic, and in many cases had hearts pierced with arrows alongside them. The concierge unlocked the doors to reveal a series of heavily ornate silver-gilt onion-domed cases inscribed with Hebrew, inside which were the yellowing scrolls of the Torah. In the top of one of them was a plastic rose.

The only other synagogue I had seen in Syria was the beautiful second-century one which had been removed piece by piece from Dura Europa, the Roman town discovered by chance by a British expeditionary force in 1920. It had been reconstructed in the thirties in the National Museum, where it could still be seen, its unique murals colourfully depicting all the great dramas of Jewish history in a bold, primitive style, like some early Aaron Spelling movie. It was now kept under lock and key, ostensibly to protect the murals from daylight, although a trustee of the museum had told me that the prime reason was to stop undercover Israeli agents photographing them for their own purposes – another example of the paranoia that hung over Damascus.

Murad was in a hurry to leave, as he had to open his shop at four o'clock. We drove back to the town centre. I popped into the bar at the Damascus International Hotel to see how Caroline had got on

with the Minister of Culture, Dr al-Attar, who was due to make a
commitment regarding the funding of the opera. Everyone was abuzz
with excitement. The normally unassuming Caroline had apparently
thrown a tantrum after the rehearsal when it became clear that the
minister was not going to commit herself after all. Caroline had not
felt it possible to continue without the money firmly in place, and
had dramatically cancelled a scheduled photo shoot to underline her
point. The tactic had been successful, and millions of Syrian pounds
had been virtually issued on the spot. I regarded Caroline in a new
light thereafter – this dainty woman wrestling with the massed forces
of the Syrian system. 'Oh, it's all part of the job,' she said self-depre-
catingly.

That evening I was due to meet Gunde to see a Franco-Syrian film
about the history of a family in the Golan Heights. The cinema was
a completely intact masterpiece of sixties interior design. Gunde was
waiting for me in the foyer. We had a drink in the café before the
film started, and I told her about Jihad. She said, 'You know, this is
a typical case. Your friend is only thirty-three, which may seem
young to you and me, but he has probably been fighting since the age
of six. My husband was attending demonstrations from the age of
twelve, or carrying letters, acting as a messenger to different parties.
The Palestinians gave everything they could for the struggle: the
women even sold their hair. Many men gave up their careers and
now they can do nothing, everything they knew is outdated. At the
end of their active lives they have nothing left. They have suffered
one defeat after another. Your friend is broken. It is very sad but
nothing unusual.'

We went in to see the film. Before it began, however, we were
shown an outdated archive film of the President opening the Assad
Library in Umawiya Square. He was wearing his long black under-
taker's overcoat and marching past rows of Baath Party officials in
black and grey suits with small knotted ties. The film took us on a
guided tour around the virgin library, which was illuminated by
extravagant chandeliers and void of humankind. It looked soulless,
lifeless, expensive. It had 'heritage' ceilings, plasterwork and fountains inside, but outside it was uncompromisingly *moderne*. The
soundtrack accompanying this inaugural visit was a lengthy eulogy
delivered by the Minister of Culture herself against a background of
the sort of sunny orchestral muzak that used to accompany adverts

for sixties holiday camps. But instead of talking about the library she was spouting a poem to the President, a paean of unalloyed praise. No doubt when the opera house was completed a similar film would be made. I wondered which lucky director would be awarded the job.

18

The English Will Give You Everything

To my surprise, I became an expert at finding Jihad's place, picking my way through the back streets by instinct. I went there every night, as if propelled by some terrible compulsion, despite the terror exerted over me by the electric bed and the potential threat of the secret police. Every time I vowed never to go back, told myself that the risks were too great, but still I would find myself trotting along the mysterious alleyways again, under the arches, through one of the old city gates (I never knew which one) with its heavy Arabic inscription, like a terrier sensing its way home. Always I wore my cap pulled down over my eyes to avoid attention. Nonetheless, the journey felt as if I were going home, and I always reached my destination with a sense of relief. For all the insecurities surrounding them, my meetings with Jihad afforded me a sense of peace, shelter and reassurance.

That night I found Jihad cooking a huge cauldron of vegetables on his electric ring. I always avoided the bed when the ring was in action and sat on the frail sofa instead. He had chopped up courgettes, tomatoes and potatoes. There was no meat, as he could not afford it, but the cassoulet had been made with animal fat. He said he would keep it and reheat it for the next two to three days. I tried to explain that it was healthier to use olive oil, and probably cheaper too. 'Ah, I have oil here,' he replied, reaching for a screw-top jar of pale green oil from an obscure source. 'It is very good for the hair.'

He was teaching me Arabic with great dedication. It was interesting watching his face when I made a mistake, and the way in which his eyes would harden into a glare of admonition, as only an Arab's eyes can, until I managed to get the phrase right. He never asked for money or a favour, or tried to exploit me in any way. Sometimes, in the café behind the mosque where he would take me to see the *hakawati* performing, he might say in front of his friends in Arabic, 'Go on. I'm tired of waiting. Tell the waiter I want another cup of tea,' and I would have to trot into the café and order the tea. His friends were staggered that this (to them) superior, rich, independent European should run at the beck and call of a prematurely broken, virtually unemployed outcast. But it was just a way of showing that ours was an understanding beyond the deferential visitor/host kind, a sort of conspiracy. Besides, it's always nice to be of service.

Despite his poverty, Jihad's latest indulgence was buying ear studs. Every few days or so he would show me yet another acquisition made during his wanderings in the souk. In addition to the pale blue one there were now also green, dark blue and gold studs, and he always gave me one of the pair as a keepsake (ironically, one pair was made in England). When I left I gave him all mine in return.

That evening, the stew having been dispensed with, we were enjoying a post-prandial cigarette and listening to the news on the World Service. The announcer's voice hailed from another era, when presenters changed into dinner jackets to read the evening news. In the middle of the bulletin the announcer would say: 'This news comes to you in the World Service of the BBC.' It was a quaint ritual which I never understood and did not wish to question. Suddenly there was a noise outside the door, which made my heart leap. Jihad got up and pulled his shirt on. 'It's OK. No problem,' he said, failing to reassure me – this was how he responded to any occurrence that had the potential to set my nerves on edge. He moved slowly over to the door with his languorous macho walk, undid the chain and went out. I heard voices in the courtyard and felt a pang of apprehension.

After a while he returned, sat down next to me on the electric bed and announced simply, 'My uncle is coming.' He had lifted up the door and propped it to one side. There was a long pause followed by a scrabbling noise, and then an individual so dirty, ragged and deformed that I felt uncomfortable, almost voyeuristic, just looking at him appeared before us, suspended on crutches. His legs were not only paralysed but shattered, dangling helplessly like those of a broken marionette. He threw one crutch onto the floor and with the other wheeled round and, leaning heavily against the door frame, slid to the ground so that he was sitting on the doorstep with his back to us. He then began to crawl like a baby across the floor, painfully slowly, dragging his dead legs behind him, until he reached the pile of rags in the corner, at which point he collapsed on his side, heaved his body up into a sitting position, and pulled his legs, one after the other, into a cross-legged stance in front of him. I wondered why Jihad had not helped him, but then I realized that the old man's pride would not permit him to do so. It was humiliating enough for him to be dragged from house to car and from car to mosque (where apparently he sat on the floor selling cheap worry beads all day), before being ferried back to the camp in the evening. Tonight he would be staying with Jihad on the pile of rags, which was his occasional home. Apart from a few staccato enquiries there was no more communication between Jihad and his uncle, who looked at me with what I took to be utter disdain.

Later Jihad's shy younger brother Saher arrived with the Syrian merchant who drove the uncle into town. The latter was a jolly, vigorous man, an amateur thespian, coarse, witty, ebullient – an entertainer. He asked me about the chances of divorce between Emir Charles and Emira Diana (all the Arabs adore Diana, whom they regard as a sort of fairytale princess-cum-prostitute figure), and about the peace process in Northern Ireland and whether I thought it would last. Finally he wanted to know about the *hibbayeen* (hippies), and if we were all still making free love in London. There was an exchange between Jihad and his uncle in which Jihad appeared to be disputing the latter's assertion. He turned to me and said, 'He says you English are incredible. First you will suck my penis like a puppy and then you will suck the breasts of a woman like a little calf. You English will have anything.'

The Arabs are notoriously frank and unashamed about sexual transactions, which are regarded in a purely practical light, as a convenience, one need meeting another. Sexual opportunity in the Middle East is highly proscribed, cynical, fleeting, purely reflexive and exploitative. That is why the true homosexual in Arab culture is so desperately lonely – other men see him as nothing more than an opportunity. No wonder that the Arab who has some emotional investment in his homosexuality cannot wait to find a European lover.

There was a lull in the conversation, and then the merchant pointed at Jihad's uncle, perched on his pile of filthy rags like a character in a Beckett play, and shouted, 'Sakespikair! That is Sakespikair!' I thought at first that he was alluding to Shakespeare, but could not, struggle as I might, make any connection between the Bard and this tragic vision in front of me. Was he some mute inglorious Lear figure? Henry after the Battle of Agincourt? The merchant repeated the word again and again, and eventually I grasped his meaning. This spectacle of human wreckage, he was saying, was the result of the Sykes-Picot agreement made secretly in 1915 between England, France and imperial Russia to decide the fate of the Ottoman Empire after the war. Under its terms, rather than granting the Arabs the independence they had promised, they carved up Turkey, the Levant and Iraq for themselves. The Arabs learned what had happened only when the Bolsheviks published the details of these plans, and they were incensed. This is the consequence of your country's diplomacy, the merchant was saying. Take a bloody good look.

The merchant and Jihad's brother left us. The former pumped my hand up and down vigorously and slapped me across the back. Everyone was suddenly laughing, including the uncle. 'Shami! Shami!' they cried. 'He is from Damascus. What can you expect?'

Jihad and his uncle had a brief conversation before the latter collapsed onto his rags and fell asleep. Jihad turned to me and said, 'My uncle says the English are cold and they are mean and inhospitable. I told him that if you visit them they will give you everything, the English: a place to sleep, friendship, welcome, money, food.' Oh dear.

It was high time to leave. My hotel was often locked by twelve o'clock and I really did not see that it was possible to stay on with the uncle lying in a heap in the corner of the room.

'Please stay. Sleep here with me tonight,' begged Jihad in his most entreating manner.

'I can't,' I said in a stage whisper.

'Why you can't?' he asked innocently.

'Well, I would have thought it was obvious. Because of him. Your uncle.'

'Oh, him. No problem.'

'It may be no problem for you,' I hissed, 'but it's a hell of problem for me.' This was putting it mildly. The electric bed, the police, and now a legless uncle. 'Anyway ...' I could hear myself pouting verbally. 'He doesn't *like* me.' So there.

'He is just an old sad man,' said Jihad. 'He wants to sleep. Listen. Can you not hear that sound?' There was a pronounced pig-like snuffling emanating from the heap of rags. 'Tomorrow you must write down this word,' Jihad went on, reaching to pull the wires from the socket. 'Snor-ring. Soon like you and me.'

I lay in bed with Jihad. As my eyes became accustomed to the dark, I looked over at the figure slumbering in the corner, wondering what the hell he thought was going on. As my eyes focused I got a sudden shock: he was the first person I had ever seen in my life who snored with his eyes open.

19

Their Names

The time had come to leave Damascus. I took a bus to Shahhaba, the show town of Philip, the only Arab Roman emperor. It had been his memorial to himself, and was now a pretty town standing on a hill, where the air was thin and cool, dwarfed by its ruins, its past. The original gates survived at each end of the street, and the theatre, palace and baths stood in solemn black tottering piles of basalt. The whole of southern Syria – before the invention of concrete, that is – was built in this mournful dark stone which had been expectorated from the numerous and now extinct volcanoes that dotted the region.

From Shahhaba I took a hop-hop into the fertile Jebel Druze and visited the village of Shaqqa, which, like the Christian village visible across the valley, stood on the top of a volcano. It contained some wonderful Byzantine villas, still inhabited by the local Druze families. One of the more splendid was large and black with a great turret, and was thought to have been a monastery. It was now occupied by a farmer, whose wife and four handsome daughters warmly beckoned me in for tea. The old women of the village still wore high-waisted Victorian-looking dresses in black damask silk and very long transparent white gauze veils which came almost to the ground, but it was not uncommon to see them walking through the village accompanying their daughters, who would be wearing blue jeans and platform sandals, their thick, long wavy hair uncovered.

The next day I set off for Bosra, calling in at Ezraa to see the huge fifth-century Byzantine church *en route*. From Ezraa I took a succession of buses to Deraa, where, somewhat exhausted, I located the Bosra bus and collapsed at a table in a nearby café. At the next table was a young man about nineteen years old, with very neatly cut black hair *en brosse* and a good-looking, blunt-featured face. He sported a designer beard and was wearing black jeans and T-shirt. He raised his head as I sat down and looked at me sulkily through narrow eyes, drawing on a Marlboro cigarette.

The driver of one of the buses leaned out of the door and gabbled in Arabic. The boy looked at me and said in English, 'You go to Bosra?' Yes, I replied, I go to Bosra. 'Come,' said the boy. I followed meekly as a lamb.

The little bus crawled through the prairies – endless fields dotted with women working on their knees in colourful clothes. Occasionally I caught a glimpse of the odd man, slumped under a tree or in a makeshift sun shelter, or perched on a tractor ploughing up and down the fields, but by and large the workforce seemed to be entirely female.

The boy told me that his name was Ahmed, and that he was a male nurse in a hospital in Deraa, where he had just finished an eighteen-hour shift. Despite this he very gallantly insisted on showing me the famous theatre in Bosra, which in the twelfth century had been encased in the doughty Ayubbid fort which still protects it today. At the same time the auditorium had been filled in with sand, thus preserving it for posterity. The theatre, now excavated, was built of basalt, but the cream marble of the stage stood out against it like a Roman palace. As I stood in the amphitheatre I tried to envisage *Dido and Aeneas* being performed there under a warm starlit Syrian sky. What could be more beautiful?

We strolled along the main street, the Cardo Maximus, taking in the ruined black buildings on the way. Some contained small houses, painted white around the doors, in which peasant families lived, with chickens scratching around the courtyard in the dirt. This Roman town was still inhabited, but I wondered if one day the Syrians would do what I had heard the Jordanians had done to the residents of Petra: build a modern housing estate around the corner and evict the local residents so that tourists could enjoy complete access to this remarkable cultural site, finally barren of all human life. It was of course the ordinary human life among the rubble which made the sight so remarkable.

We finally reached the end of the Cardo Maximus in something of a state of exhaustion. It was very hot. We were both shattered and I had burned knees (I had now caved in to the desire to feel comfortable and had decided to flaunt convention by wearing my shorts. The reaction I got was as if I had walked down Oxford Street in a kilt.) We waited for what seemed an age for a bus, sitting in the niche of the western gate. 'Tomorrow we go to see the Mosque of the Kneeling Camel,' murmured Ahmed feebly. 'Tonight you stay with me.' All right by me, I thought. This is what is wonderful about travel – it enables you to be so deliciously passive, blown willy-nilly hither and yon. Come day, go day. Nothing really matters.

I trudged across the road to a shop and bought some cans of revivifying Coke from a woman with a bishop's mitre and a gold tooth. Eventually the bus hove into view. Several miles down the road, Ahmed made it stop outside a large house standing in a neglected garden. We walked down the garden path and into the house. Unusually, it transpired, Ahmed was an only child whose father had died when he was young, and he had been brought up single-handedly by his mother, who nearly fainted clean away to see an *ajnabee* wearing shorts standing in her kitchen. Later, Ahmed told me that she had never met a European before me. I felt like an exotic fruit.

Ahmed took me into the *majlis*, which, as in so many Syrian houses, was a very simple affair – a large room with virtually no furniture, just mattresses round the walls interspersed with stacks of hard cushions against which one could lean. We sat down and chatted about his English lessons and he fetched an old and battered dictionary to facilitate conversation. Much time was spent riffling backwards and forwards through the pages to help clarify the logjam of meanings that we could not express. I put my head against a cushion and stretched out. I realized that I was absolutely exhausted – glutted with new impressions and experiences, drained by the incredible heat, riddled with the stress of travel and the paranoia that seemed to be a feature of a visit to Syria. I felt my eyelids closing. Ahmed was stroking my hair, as though I were a strange form of lapdog. His arm fell against my chest and we fell asleep in each other's arms.

We were woken by a rap on the door. Ahmed sat up with a start and went to open it. His mother, who had prepared some tea and food, was standing there respectfully, not daring to burst in on our sacrosanct male social intercourse.

'After eat, sleep,' Ahmed said, returning with a tray.

'Fine. After eat, sleep,' I parroted.

It was all so simple. We ate. We slept. I stayed for days.

* * *

all along the bank were young men fishing, swimming and playing in the water. Often, on Fridays, they would appear on the suspension bridge, dressed in shorts and rugby tops, and as a dare hurl themselves into the swirling water below. At night from the bridge I saw glorious sunsets, the huge sky smeared with gold and purple streaks.

As well as being somehow traditional and conservative in terms of its ethnic population, the fact that Syria's richest oilfields were near by meant that there was something of a forward-looking lifestyle about the place. There were sleazy bars where posters of nude women adorned the walls, and upriver was a Sheraton where all the rich, bored European engineers stayed, frittering away their substantial salaries on expensive drinks in its bar. There was also a large and restive proportion of the population hostile to the government. They listened to Iraqi radio, received Iraqi TV and spoke Arabic with an Iraqi accent. The air of dissent was refreshing and welcome.

I checked in to a wonderful white 1930s hotel, the Raghdan, built overlooking the river. The large detached building retained an aura of thirties glamour, its design quite clearly inspired by an ocean liner. Indeed it reminded me of one, standing in its moorings by the river. It cost only sixteen dollars a night and was, for the price, very clean and comfortable. For the first time since I left the Baron I had an *en suite* bathroom and a pink loo all to myself. It had *proper* beds with sprung mattresses and no bed bugs, endless hot water, a desk and an easy chair. Bliss.

I became friendly with a young man called Suleyman who worked in a nearby hotel that I had inspected but could not afford. He had directed me to the Raghdan, and appeared later after work to show me around. When he arrived I was lying prone on my bed under the fan. Outside the heat was simply colossal – we were apparently in the middle of a heatwave. He spoke good English and begged me to leave the hotel and stay with him, but I had had enough of hospitality by this time. I wanted to be alone – to sprawl in bed till God knows when and have my breakfast brought to me. I wanted to write letters and postcards to friends and indulge myself in every possible way. The last thing I wanted was to be polite. So exhausting.

I consented to visit Suleyman's house, which he described as 'a magnificent place'. On the way people threw stones at me a couple of times, but Suleyman told me not to worry about it – it was just normal behaviour. People here were not wild about Europeans after the Gulf War. Everyone in Deir es Zor had been on the side of Saddam Hussein.

The 'magnificent place' turned out to be a small modern flat in which Suleyman lived with his parents and brother, who was studying medicine in Aleppo. It was a modest middle-class abode with his father's very bad oil paintings on the walls and a slightly literary and artistic feel to it. His father was a lecturer. When we arrived he was lying on the sofa in his pyjamas, reading a book. He had long wild white hair and looked every inch the mad don. During the course of my visit there was a power cut, and the fan on the ceiling of the small room ground to a halt. Suleyman went to the balcony to open the windows but immediately closed them again. 'It is not possible to open them because of the dust storm,' he explained. I went to the window and saw what he meant – great clouds of dust were swirling along the street. Because Deir es Zor is on the edge of the desert there was a similar storm every evening. The result was that we were stuck with no electric fan and were unable to open the windows. I nearly passed out because of the heat. This, I mused, lying on the sofa like a lump of lead, is where the Arabs are so wrong to ape European building styles. The traditional Arabic house, with its system of natural draughts and its enclosed courtyard isolated from the streets (unlike these modern flats, which gave out on to them), would have been able to cope with this problem.

We all sat around feeling weak, hot and irritable, drinking chilled rosewater the colour of Turkish delight made by Suleyman's mother from distilled rose petals. Before I left, I told Suleyman that I wished to go to the Armenian memorial church. He said that he had a half-Armenian friend who could take me there. His name was Tariq, and it was into his neurotic hands that I was to fall for the remainder of my visit.

24

Dust in the Air

Of all the people I met in Syria, I found Tariq the most trying. He had a very loud voice, and everything he said he repeated twice, often three times, in order to make himself clear. He was very intelligent but extremely highly strung. He was constantly seeking to improve his English, which was already very good, although he had never been further afield than Damascus in his life. He was not an attractive fellow, of medium height and slim build with rather bulging eyes behind his specs. His complexion was poor and he had wiry hair parted to the side. He was incredibly intense and burned with an ardent and keenly felt sense of injustice at all sorts of things. He was half Armenian by virtue of having two Armenian grandparents, one on each side of the family. His maternal grandmother, a Christian Armenian, had, upon marrying a Moslem, been forced to convert and bring Tariq's own mother up a Moslem, so he too had been raised in the Moslem faith. It was his intention not only to convert to Christianity but to become a curate. The conversion would have to take place in Lebanon, but how he was going to carry out his plan was as yet unclear. He thought that maybe he would have to emigrate to Armenia; he could speak a little Armenian but he intended to improve this so that he could teach it in Syria and ensure its preservation. He was passionate about the way the Armenians had been treated in 1915 and indignant about the fact that the Syrian authorities dictated that only Arab history could be taught in schools. Furthermore, I discovered after a few days, he was not only voluble about the shortcomings of the government, but vitriolic about their corruption and inefficiency. Although I found him trying to be with, our friendship was eased by one vital and necessary factor: I held him in the highest respect. I also felt that he was trustworthy and was extremely grateful for the enormous efforts he went to on my behalf.

For many decades, if not centuries, before 1915, relations between the Armenians and the Turks (who since the tenth century had more or less controlled the huge Christian kingdom of Armenia) had been extremely bad. In the nineteenth century there was a flare-up of nationalistic activity and repeated assassinations of Ottoman officials in Istanbul. In the constant struggle between Russia and Turkey, fuelled and manipulated by the Western powers, the Armenians often aided the Russians in an attempt to throw off their much-despised Turkish oppressors. Things came to a head in the First World War when it was discovered that some of the Armenians were assisting the Russians against the Turks. This provided the perfect excuse for the Turks to deal with this refractory Christian race, which had been stuck like a thorn in the side of the Ottoman Empire for so long, once and for all. The Western powers were too busy tearing each other apart to take any effective action. (Many of the photographs of the appalling atrocities that resulted were taken by German officers – Germany was the Ottomans' ally, and has often been accused of having some role in the organization and planning of the mass killings.)

The church commemorating the massacre was situated near the river. It was a modern building, recently completed, designed in the traditional Armenian style with an octagonal tower. On the ground floor, in the middle of the room, was a column enclosed by wrought-iron railings. Encircling its base was a glass case displaying human arm, leg and skull bones.

Two staircases spiralled down to the lower floor where a small museum was devoted to the massacre (or, as the Armenians themselves refer to it, the Holocaust). Among the exhibits were some of the tragic images I had seen in the Armenian museum in Jerusalem, most memorably the picture of Armenian priests in their square hats and long black veils standing in the Syrian desert, holding bleached white bones in the shape of a cross. Framed beneath it were Hitler's sinister words about the 'final solution': 'Who remembers today the massacres of the Armenians?' It is true that it took the Armenians many years to organize an effective propaganda strategy to publicize their tragedy – a tragedy for which to this day the Turks have made no public acknowledgement or apology, let alone any form of redress. Hitler was right: few people in the West have any idea that such a massacre took place.

Tariq and I repaired to the café near my hotel. I ordered a large glass of *zorat* (flower tea). Tariq told me of a project he had long had in mind – to visit a village about fifteen kilometres away. 'There is a place there which the villagers call the Armenian Holes,' he said. 'They say that many Armenians were killed there. They were put into something like underground houses. Each house has a door and some steps down. You can find them today but they are all blocked up. I think for the Armenian community's records it should be visited. Perhaps you would like to come and explore this place with me?'

I replied that I would find such a trip very interesting, and we made an appointment to meet at eight o'clock the next morning in the hotel. Before he left, I asked if he knew of any Armenians who had survived the massacre still living near Deir es Zor who could remember what had happened. 'There are some very old people alive,' he said, 'but they survived the massacre only as infants and can remember very little, maybe nothing. Last week the Armenian ambassador awarded these people Armenian nationality as part of the eightieth anniversary memorial of the massacres, but they will never use it. As for people who are old enough to remember and are still in possession of their faculties, I will have to make enquiries. I think there is one lady who was living in a village outside Deir, a tailor and very, very old, maybe ninety-five. I will try and find out for you.'

He got on his rather battered old bike and wobbled away over the dusty, potholed streets, and I went to the hotel for a siesta.

The next morning, like all Syrian mornings, dawned with a peerless blue sky which indicated that the day would probably become very hot. Nonetheless I had noticed that occasionally, even in June, the sky here could be overcast with great dust clouds. Tariq, I discovered, welcomed such days, as they were cooler. 'Put your hands on your face and tell me what you find,' he said to me once. I followed his instructions and found that my face was covered in fine grit. 'The dust in the air protects us from the sun,' he explained.

That morning Tariq came to the hotel as arranged, and we walked over the bridge to the bustling material market on the opposite bank. This was the most colourful market I had seen in Syria, with its yards and yards of gaily coloured cloth hanging over the railings along the river, and a great cloud of country women in their multi-hued gowns and head-dresses clustering around the squares of material laid out one upon the other on the floor.

We boarded a bus bound for Madloom and headed out into the desert. About ten kilometres down the road we alighted at a nondescript place. Somewhere in the distance down a dirt track lay the village that was our destination, but around us all we could see were the oilfields, the great hope of the Syrian economy. Tariq looked at them with a sneer of disgust. 'What is the use of it all if we never see the money from it? It all goes to Damascus, into the pockets of the government, to waste and squander while we all live in poverty.'

We walked up the dirt track for a while towards the village. A little boy, about eight years old, came trotting towards us daintily on a white donkey. He was wearing a crisp pale grey djellabah and had short-cropped dark blond hair and large almond-shaped eyes the colour of honey. Tariq asked him the whereabouts of the Gheir Armeni, the Armenian Holes. The little boy said nothing, but twisted in his saddle and gestured elegantly towards an area near the village, then kicked his donkey into motion again. 'You see,' said Tariq. 'Everyone knows the place by this name.'

We followed the direction of the boy's finger and soon noticed that the ground was becoming extremely uneven. On the surface everywhere around us were hundreds of fragments of old broken clay pottery, although the village itself was still some way off. Eventually we came to a well with a black basalt stone of Byzantine design on top of it. 'You see here under the ground was once a city,' explained Tariq. 'You must photograph this well for me. Without doubt it was where the Turks pushed in the prisoners.' I peered into the well and dropped a stone down it. It disappeared into blackness and I did not hear it land. People say that so many bodies were forced into the wells that they became polluted; some claim that after 1915 many of them dried up.

Further along we came to the first of a series of submerged doorways blocked up with sand so that only a half or a third of them was visible. Some were not visible at all, while others were quite easily accessible. 'I think this is the place,' said Tariq, scrambling down the hollow to the door. At the bottom he began kicking at the door until it caved in. Lying on his back, he slid into the hole beneath. I followed him, and we found ourselves in what I recognized to be a Roman tomb. It was a small room about five feet in height and about six feet long. On either side and in front of us, carved into the earth, were three arched niches. Tariq went over to one of them and ran his fingers across it. 'Oh God,' he murmured. 'Look what I have found.' He turned round and held up a human arm bone. I felt into the niche on my left. Inside there were more bones, very badly decomposed. 'Quickly,' said Tariq, 'we must take these bones back to the church. We have no time to lose.'

He scrambled out of the tomb and returned moments later with a handful of black plastic bags. (In Syria you are rarely far away from a plastic bag as the market produce is sold in them and they are dropped everywhere. These had blown from the village into the hollows in the ground.) We started to stuff as many bones as we could fit into the bags. 'I will take them to a doctor who will date them,' said Tariq, shovelling a few ribs into a bag, 'and then we must have them blessed in the church.' I wondered whether the poor inmates of the tomb had been killed before being stuffed inside, or whether they had been walled in to die. I tried to imagine what it would be like, dying in such a manner. Perhaps like drowning. Perhaps they died with relief. Or perhaps they were beyond it by then, their malnourished, sun-scorched bodies almost incapable of supporting any further suffering. We looked on the walls for the sign of the Cross, but none was visible, which presumably indicated that the first option was the more likely – that the Armenian deportees were in all likelihood, mercifully, dead before the tombs were sealed up.

It did not really occur to me to reflect on how I had got myself into this strange position, or upon the morality, and indeed legality, of what I was doing. It had just happened to me. Now I was here, I did what I was told. A moment had presented itself to us; we were operating within it. In many respects, life is like that in Syria. In other countries, where you have the luxury of being able to assess the pros and cons, the wider moral good, it is no doubt different. Here, in a country where so much is proscribed, you do something because it becomes suddenly possible. Looking back, I think this was partly the impetus behind my relationship with Jihad. It became suddenly – just about – possible, so it happened.

Occasionally the silence was broken by a melodramatic exhortation from Tariq. 'Quickly, quickly, Robert. If the police find us here we will be taken to prison. Ah my God, I cannot believe this. These are the bones of my grandfathers.'

I was surprised by the fragility of the bones. Some were the texture of charcoal, light, porous and crumbling. I picked up part of a human cranium and it simply crumbled away in my hands. I remembered a passage in one of the quotations pinned up in the museum about how, years after the massacre, it had become common for the Bedouin children to break into these sealed tombs and caves in order to ransack the skeletons for gold teeth or wedding rings. I remembered the mummy rags in the funerary towers of Palmyra and the grinning, mocking smile of Kallil, son of Akhenaten. Death seemed to be everywhere in this country.

We left the tomb with four plastic bags of remains and emerged blinking into the harsh desert sun. I spat on the ground. I was covered in tomb dust and my mouth and nostrils were full of it, as was my hair. The dust of dead Armenians. All around us, as we walked, we found more of the submerged doors. I realized then that we were walking above an extensive necropolis – a necropolis twice over, both Byzantine and Armenian.

Tariq said that it would be necessary to return to this spot with Armenian priests. We photographed what we could, brushed each other down, and returned to the road. After a few minutes a micro appeared and we climbed on board. Coming back into Deir es Zor, we crossed the Euphrates. After the choking dust and darkness of the underground tombs, it looked beautiful and peaceful with its lush green trees trailing into the water. I asked Tariq if we could get off and walk back to the church. He stopped the bus and we began to walk towards the river. Suddenly he said, 'Robert, where is your other bag?' I had my own bag in one hand and a bag of bones in the other. I looked at Tariq, who was holding a bag of bones in each hand, then into the distance, at the shrinking shape of the micro. 'It's on the bus,' I said apologetically.

Tariq gave me an exasperated look. 'We have to get it. It is a small mistake which could cost us dearly. If anyone finds that bag and they give it to the police and describe you they can trace you in two minutes. You could be arrested for stealing from a site of national historical importance, not to mention stirring up anti-Syrian feeling.'

'Well, don't just stand there. Let's get a taxi.'

'Half the bus and taxi drivers in this town are informers,' snapped Tariq.

'What else are supposed to do?' I gibbered. 'Run behind? If we don't get a taxi soon we've really had it.' The intense heat was adding to my increasing sense of irritation and panic.

'Indeed,' said Tariq, 'but first we must move from the sight of this building behind us.'

I looked at the beautiful old house standing in its own gardens overlooking the river. 'Why?' I asked.

'It is the headquarters for the Mukhabarat.'

'Jesus,' I said, shuffling after Tariq towards the roundabout beyond which the bus had disappeared.

Almost on cue, a yellow car rattled around the roundabout and I flagged it down. It was shaped like a jelly mould, a cartoon car. We got in and Tariq told a lie about the *ajnabee* leaving his bag full of important travel documents on the bus. We sped along the road, and each time we approached a micro we overtook it and leered at all the passengers and the driver. 'What did the driver look like, Robert?' Tariq asked.

'I don't know. Fat. Middle-aged with a moustache,' I replied. All the drivers of the micros were fat, middle-aged and moustachioed.

Eventually we reached the terminus and paid off the taxi. We wandered around with our remaining bones and asked about the bus that had come in from Madloom. But people said either that they did not know its whereabouts or that it had just left. I was feeling hot and bothered by this stage, and went to a café, sat down and ordered a gazeuse for each of us. Tariq dumped his bones on a chair next to me and disappeared. I found myself wondering how many pieces of how many people were in the missing bag, thinking what a strange posthumous existence they were now leading.

After a while Tariq returned, wreathed in smiles. In his hand was the fourth bag, knotted securely at the top. 'Where did you find it?' I asked, too hot even to feel relief.

'Some people told me that the bus for Madloom stops behind the terminus to fill up with passengers before it goes back,' he said. 'I ran round and got there just as it was leaving. Someone had given the bag to the driver. It was under his seat.'

'What did he say about the bones?'

'He just said, "What sort of strange young man are you to collect old stones and rocks," and that was all. We are very lucky.'

He collapsed on a chair and swigged his gazeuse. Later we walked back into town, and Tariq left me to find the doctor who could verify and date the bones, saying he would come to the hotel at about eight that evening.

25

'I Am for Iraq'

I took a stroll through the souk, which reminded me of a cathedral, with its high arched, ribbed roof and its cruciform design. There was a sizable offal section giving off an appalling stench: noses, eyes, heads, tongues and piles of guts were everywhere. At the opposite end I found an old man selling jewellery, but the moment he saw me he increased his prices tenfold. They ranged from ten to two hundred and fifty dollars a piece, and it was exactly the sort of stuff that Gladys had been buying up in sackloads to tart up and flog off in Manhattan. At the other end of the covered bazaar, I came upon a beautiful Ottoman gateway with the Toura, the Ottoman insignia, above it. It had previously been the main gate of the Turkish Army's headquarters. Now it was filled in with breeze block.

I walked on to the museum. Outside it was an old man with an incredibly ancient camera – the sort with a black hood under which he had to disappear to take a photograph. His subjects had to sit on a packing case against the museum wall. Inside, I was alarmed to find that the entrance fee had gone up to ten dollars. It was a ridiculous charge considering that all the finds from Babylonian Mari and Seleucid Doura Europos, the two major sites in the vicinity, were in either Damascus or Paris. I decided not to risk the collections of shop dummies clad in local garb and stuffed birds which I guessed were inside. By the ticket office was a young American woman, imaginatively dressed with dark brown hair in a pretty Heidi plait and lovely if unnerving green eyes. We started to compare notes about whether or not it was worth paying the entrance fee and decided it wasn't. Instead we repaired to the café across the road, next to my hotel.

Her name was Ginny. She was English-born but raised in the States, whither her father – a scientist – had emigrated during the brain drain of the seventies. She hated America, but having been brought up there was stuck with an accent she could not stand. At university she had read Middle Eastern culture and Arabic and she had spent a year in Cairo. She was staying with a 'friend' in the five-star Ferat Al Cham Hotel outside town. The friend was an American called Dwight. He was teaching English to oil workers and she was sharing his bedroom. It turned out that she had a card in her pocket from the Rose of Aleppo with my name written on the back, given to her by some students I had met in Palmyra. She was intending to go to the Rose later with Dwight to continue what she seemed to regard as her holiday romance, though I guessed she was the sort of girl who fell on her feet rather than in love. She had a wonderfully ironic manner and a sense of independence and detach-ment which I quite liked, but like a lot of single women travelling alone in the Middle East she had a toughness about her that was very soon to become apparent.

'Do you know what's happening here at the moment?' she asked me. I confessed I did not.

'There's a huge oil spillage. A leak in one of the well casings. There is an enormous lake outside town. We drove round it last night. Everyone here is terrified. They think if it gets any hotter there could be a terrific explosion.' She explained that various American experts had been called in, and that they were looking at ways of sinking more wells to draw off the excess oil. 'The problem is it's all supposed to be top secret. There's nothing on the news about it. But everyone in this town is scared shitless, although they reckon the town itself is safe – the spill is about fifteen kilometres away, but it's getting bigger every day.'

We agreed to meet for breakfast at my hotel the next day, and I sent her off to see the Armenian ossuary (she knew nothing about the Armenian saga). I, meanwhile, went back to the hotel and showered the bone dust out of my hair before taking a long nap.

At 8.30 a.m. the phone rang as I was writing my diary. It was the surly receptionist downstairs. He told me my friend Tariq was in reception. 'Send him up, please,' I said, and returned to my lucubra-tions. After a while I realized there was still no Tariq and stomped downstairs looking for him. I found him sitting in the foyer. 'Tariq, what are you doing there?' I demanded, somewhat shortly. 'I asked them to send you upstairs fifteen minutes ago.'

He rolled his eyes. 'They won't allow me upstairs,' he muttered.

'Nonsense. Come with me,' I snapped huffily, looking as imperiously as I could at the lout lolling behind the desk (I have always had a predilection for baiting minor officials). It was the beginning of a degenerating relationship with the hotel authorities. We disappeared through the swing doors.

'Robert, you must be careful,' said Tariq as we mounted the stairs. 'All these people in the hotels report to the Mukhabarat. Everywhere you are being watched. I am being watched. When you are out they will come here and photograph everything – your diary, your book. They are writing about you. The man told me it was not allowed for me to go upstairs. He said it was not allowed for me even to talk to you. We have to go downstairs now and say goodbye to each other. Then you will leave the hotel twenty minutes later and meet me on the far side of the bridge. I know a nice restaurant by the river. OK?'

In the foyer we went through an elaborate farewell ceremony.

'Well, goodbye, Tariq, and thank you so much for your help. I will not forget your kindness,' I proclaimed, enunciating all my words with Am. Dram. exaggeration for the benefit of the reception-ist. 'And don't worry. I shall certainly be writing to you from England. Goodbye. Goodbye.' I waved vigorously and disappeared back up the stairs.

Back in my room I sat at my desk and looked at all my effects. Had they been tampered with? Were they being photographed? Were they reading my diaries? Surely not. No one – not even myself – could read my diaries. I wondered about gluing a hair across the gap between door and frame to see if it was still there when I came back. No, I decided. I was getting paranoid.

I left the hotel and crossed the bridge. Tariq was waiting for me. His eyes were bulging. 'You do not understand what it is like here,' he said peevishly. 'Keep walking and don't look behind you.'

'Why not?' I asked, automatically swivelling my head and gog-gling behind me the way you do when told not to look at something.

'I am being followed. Don't look!' Tariq hissed.

We walked across the central island to the graceful suspension bridge. Outside a dilapidated house a young mother and her friend were sitting with their legs stretched out in the dust. Next to them, lying on a towel, was a baby. Every night as I passed this house I saw the same group. I could not understand why they would want to sit there with a baby in the dust and the fumes and the filth being churned up by the passing traffic.

On the suspension bridge, Tariq stopped. 'Wait here and you will see what I mean,' he said.

We gazed over the river and its islands into the distance, watching the sun sink slowly into the horizon. 'OK, look to your right now.' I looked and saw two men also leaning over the bridge. They were in civilian clothes, but round their waists – in the style of the 'presidential guard' in Damascus – they each had a belt with a small black pistol. When we walked on and stopped, they walked on and stopped. On the far side of the river, we walked past the swimming pool and entered the park. The men entered the park too. 'What does it mean?' I asked Tariq.

He shrugged. 'They are very suspicious here,' he explained. 'You see, my brother-in-law was taken to prison during the war. The war with Iraq. Everyone here was on the side of Iraq. Everyone. Apart from the Baath Party.'

'Why did they take him?'

'Someone heard him. An informer. All he said was, "I am on the side of Iraq." That is all. Then they came one night and they took him. He went to an underground prison, a terrible place. Far from here – Damascus.' (No one could say the word Damascus with quite the venom with which Tariq could say it. He usually used the Arabic name, Dimashq, ending with an impressive glottal.) 'They kept him there for one year. We did not know where he was. We were terrified – the whole family. If one person is taken they can take another as a form of blackmail – maybe the wife or daughter. Maybe the elder son. For example, the man who they have taken may have a son studying at the university. One day they come. They come with guns. They march into the lecture hall. He is taken, gone. Never seen again. Maybe he is killed. Maybe he is let out after six months. Maybe six years. You never, ever know. It happens all the time. Robert, I am going to tell you the number of that prison. They all have a number. I want you to remember it. My brother-in-law was in this place for one year. They beat him. On the soles of his feet. They put him in the folding chair.'

'What's that?'

'It is awful. Terrible. You must sit in it and the back folds. They can break your back with this if they want. He lived on dry bread and one cup of water a day. But the water and the bread were served at different ends of the day. He could not digest the bread. He could not chew it even. His mouth was so dry and swollen but they forced him to eat it. After a while he could not walk because of the beatings. He had cracks in the soles of his feet. He could not go to the toilet. He was … How do you say when you cannot go to the toilet?'

'Constipated.'

'Yes. Constipated. Exactly. He was constipated. Very badly. He spent months in agony. He is not political. He is not a member of a banned political party. Thank God. All he said was in this war "I am for Iraq." Like everyone in this town. He would not tell us where this prison was. Or anything about it. All he would say was that it was a terrible place somewhere beneath the ground near Dimashq.'

We strolled around the park and took a gazeuse at the café overlooking the river. 'Do you think they've gone now?' I asked.

'No,' replied Tariq. 'They are sitting over there on the bench. It is their method. Maybe they will go soon. They like to frighten people.'

We walked back over the bridge and found a restaurant on the far bank. Lights hung in the trees and a cat hung around watching me eat the chicken I had ordered. I gave her most of it, and she ran off with it in her mouth to the little shed where her kittens were. Tariq smiled at her scrawny frame and regarded the carcass on my plate. 'Robert, why have you not given it to her to eat?'

'I don't think it's a good idea,' I said. 'She might choke on the bones.'

'In her life she has already dealt with far worse problems. Give it to her.'

I dropped the carcass on the floor and the mother cat snatched it up and scuttled away under the tables to her young.

'By the way, with regard to the bones,' said Tariq. 'The doctor dated them between eighty and a hundred years old, which means they are as far as we can prove Armenian. I took them to the church and the father will bless them. He sends his thanks and regards to you. And there is one favour he requires of you. When you go back to Aleppo, can you take a box of the remains to the priest there? They want to put some in the church.'

'Fine. No problem,' I replied. (Dem bones. Dem bones. Would I ever be rid of them?)

I chucked the last scraps of chicken onto the floor. Tariq looked at the cat and then at me. 'You know,' he said, 'here in Syria our lives are worse than that of an animal in Europe.'

We left the restaurant and strolled along the dark, deserted street. On the bridge Tariq went one way and I another. We did not see the men with the guns again.

26

Israel's Secret Weapon

I spent the next few mornings touring the local countryside. In the afternoons, poleaxed by a heat I had never experienced before, I vegetated in the hotel, fantasizing about the green, green grass of home. Occasionally I found myself quite swamped with overpowering feelings of longing for England – England, where everything was so mild and ordered and urbane. From my borrowed vantage point, England seemed an infinitely richer, more complex, more highly evolved, more experimental, more cultured society than the one I was languishing in now. I wanted to go home. The Armenian stuff was getting to me. I had let myself get very run down – my nerves were in tatters; I had ulcers on my tongue. I only had to hear Big Ben on the World Service and I would crack up.

Most days I would meet up with Ginny for breakfast or tea. She was being swished around the country in her lover's car. She never offered me a lift or included me in her plans. If, however, I went on a trip with Tariq, I always invited her and she always accepted, and then usually got stroppy about getting home to meet Dwight after work. Tariq had obviously fallen headlong in love with her, and every night we had to visit the only one of his friends who had a phone so that we could ring the Ferat Al Cham and talk to her. The friend was a bodybuilder, a dashing young man who looked like an Arab prince, with the thin downy moustache of a thirties film star and moist eyelashes and soft black eyes – so black they appeared almost bottomless. He worked as a chemist, but whenever I met him he was strutting around in tracksuit bottoms and a skimpy vest. He was called Naim, and he longed to travel and live in Europe. He asked me how he might achieve this ambition. I could think of only one way that had the faintest hope of success, and said, 'Have you met my friend Ginny?' I rather hoped to tear Ginny away from the American and set her up with the beauteous Naim. She was obviously

sexually quite generous, and surely she would not be able to resist such a picture of male Arabic beauty as Naim presented. There were only two flaws to my master plan. Firstly, what was in it for Ginny, other than a few bonks? I seriously doubted that she was capable of altruism. Secondly, Tariq.

Tariq's face was a picture as I outlined my plan. He looked most put out. Even the fact that Ginny was Jewish did not deter him from his infatuation. All Syrians live in terror of Israelis infiltrating their country. The most famous such story concerns Eli Cohen, the Israeli spy who became close to the President and was informing on the Syrians for years before his discovery and subsequent public execution. The Syrians know that there is nothing they can do to stop American and European Jews visiting their country if their names are sufficiently Anglicized on their passports, and they do not like it at all. It was to his credit, therefore, that Ginny's Jewishness did not deter Tariq from pressing his suit. He had seen her name on her passport when she was cashing some cheques at the bank. That evening he said to me, 'The name Abrahams. It is Jewish, is it not?' I did not then know what Ginny's religion was, but she had told me that her family had come from eastern Europe after the war, so I imagined that she must have been of Jewish extraction. 'I really do not know what it is, Tariq,' I said casually.

Naim and Tariq then had a protracted discussion. Tariq turned to me and said, 'We Syrians are frightened of Jewish women.'

'Really? Why is that?'

'They all carry AIDS.'

I asked him on what basis he was making this allegation.

'It is well known. And it has been in all the papers.'

'I thought you thought your newspapers were full of lies,' I countered.

'It has been on the TV too,' replied Tariq. 'Do you not know the famous story of how Israel sent three beautiful Jewish women prostitutes to Egypt and they slept with all the high officials in the Egyptian government and now they all have AIDS?'

I had to confess that I had missed this wonderful tale of the viral Mata Haris. Perhaps, like the story of the oil in Windsor Great Park, it too would turn out to be true.

In the mornings, when I was free, I swam in the Bassel Al Assad swimming pool. Generally I went when it was closed and did the white sahib bit, throwing my money around so that the lifeguards put the place at my disposal. The normal price was ten Syrian pounds but I, being a bloated plutocrat, paid fifty (roughly a dollar) and for that had the whole place to myself for an hour before opening time. To swim on my own in the open air by the Euphrates in a vast, cool swimming pool in the devastating heat was almost perfection.

Sometimes I would bump into the local swimming stars, some of whom represented their country in international competitions. Compared to the Arab kids who splashed around in there normally, these prime specimens looked like the warrior youths of the Elgin Marbles come to life, back and abdominal muscles rippling with beads of water as they heaved themselves out of the pool and rested inert on the side like a pride of lions sunning themselves. They wore expensive shades and skimpy European swimwear that they had bought on their travels. They were the favoured sons. A race apart.

When the pool was open to the public, I would lie on the side with my favourite swimmer. He was a polio victim and was, his withered leg aside, rather a handsome fellow. He had been in all sorts of disabled sporting events, including one in London, where he had had the misfortune to stay in Northwood Hills and see only the inside of a Hertfordshire pool.

Around us, hordes of local youths swarmed into the water, turning the pool into a jacuzzi of mayhem. The Arabs are very bad swimmers. It has never been part of their culture, and like the prudish Victorians they wear a strange assortment of garb in which to bathe: pantaloons, shorts, T-shirts, baseball caps, tracksuit bottoms, football kit – anything billowing. They swim like wind-up plastic toys, heads held out of the water, moving alternately to right and left with each stroke.

Tariq had managed to track down the name and address of the Armenian woman who had survived the massacre. She was now apparently living on a farm in the countryside outside Deir es Zor. We decided to visit her, and the three of us (Tariq, Ginny and I, who were now lurching around together like the Three Stooges) met at the bus station early in the morning before it became too hot. While we waited for the bus, Tariq made enquiries about the lady, who was called Umm Ahmed, among fellow travellers. Sometimes he would come back looking solemn and say, 'She is dead.' Other times he looked delighted and told us, 'No, she is still alive.' Nobody seemed to know what the situation was.

We lingered on the bus, waiting for it to fill up. A small boy walked down the gangway selling ice lollies in plastic packets. I bought one each for Ginny and me, and we used them, much to the surprise of the country women on the bus, as ice packs, sliding them against our foreheads, the backs of our necks, down our shirts. When they had thoroughly melted the boy came up to us and, demonstrating no little entrepreneurial flair, flogged us another two, taking back the original ones and plopping them into his bucket to refreeze and sell on to other customers.

'We had a most interesting conversation last night, didn't we, Tariq?' I remarked. 'Tariq has the ultimate conspiracy theory,' I recounted to Ginny, 'about how the Egyptian government is being wiped out by being seduced by a plague of Israeli AIDS-infested prostitutes.' It sounded quite biblical in the retelling.

Ginny showed no reaction, but looked at Tariq and said coolly, 'What really happens is that all those rich government officials spend all their holidays having sex jags with prostitutes in Thailand. When I lived in Cairo people talked about it all the time. They've got to find someone to blame.'

The country women around us seemed, I thought, to be dressed most inappropriately for the weather, with layers and layers of robes and shawls, the outermost of which, when necessary, was hooked up in the hands and used as a sort of sack, stuffed with goodness knows what. The materials were all artificial, and many of the women, unbelievably, wore rubber shoes *and* nylons of some description. There we were, meanwhile, in expensive, cool, pale Nicole Fahri linen, rubbing ice lollies all over our bodies. One of the women watching us was a leathery dame in her middle years. Under her bottom lip two long blue triangles had been tattooed. They looked like fangs.

The village was not far away. When we alighted Tariq had to go through the same process of enquiry as at the bus station. As Ginny and I stood waiting for him to come back with directions, a long crocodile of young girls marched past us on their way to work in the fields. They wore many-layered gowns and multicoloured headscarves tied over their heads and faces in such a way as to reveal only their eyes. Over each shoulder they carried a pick. *Landmadchens* going to till the land. From a distance they looked terribly sinister, like terrorists. But as they passed me I became aware of the beauty of their long almond eyes with their feathery lashes, out of which some of them looked shyly, others apprehensively, others curiously. None of them held my gaze for more than a split second.

We were taken to a nearby house belonging to an Armenian family. There were, Tariq had discovered, eight Armenian families in this village. Here we were told that Umm Ahmed had indeed died, only six weeks previously. Her descendants, including children from two marriages, grandchildren and great-grandchildren, were said to number approximately 250. All of them were Moslems. The family we were talking to was also completely Moslem. The paterfamilias had married an Armenian girl, but both were descended from Armenians who had converted to avoid liquidation. Their children were pure Armenian, but spoke not one word of their language. They wore djellabahs and keffiyehs and the men all toyed carelessly with their worry beads when we spoke. They sat on the floor on cushions, served us rose juice and ate with their right hands. We had to take our shoes off before entering their home. Their identities had been completely changed. If the Turks had set out to break a race, then in these Armenians and others like them they had succeeded. I asked the old man if he wanted to find out about his family history, and he said that it had never really occurred to him to do so. All he knew was that his parents had met in Deir after the massacre. They had survived, and he had a difficult enough living to make as it was, bringing up his many children, without thinking about the past.

One of the sons of the family installed us in a trezeena and transported us to the farmstead where Umm Ahmed had lived. It was a beautiful smallholding set in fertile farmland, a little paradise surrounded by willows and poplars, palms and huge oleander bushes covered in pale pink flowers. We were received by Ahmed, Umm Ahmed's eldest son and now the owner of the smallholding, in the courtyard of their house. He was happy to tell us the story of his mother's long life and invited us into his *majlis*. He was surrounded by his blond-haired sons, some of whom were now at university, and his granddaughters. With his pot belly and long, rounded nose, he looked like every Armenian you have ever seen, except that he was wearing a djellabah and turban and, again, he could not speak the language.

Before he started to tell us about his mother, he produced an old axe. He said that it had been given to her on the march through the desert, and he drew our attention to the symbols on each side of it, consisting of a series of arrows and crosses. The arrows traced the routes of the deportations from Armenia in eastern Turkey through the desert, and the crosses the sites of the atrocities at which the Armenian martyrs (for such is how they refer to those who were killed) had died. His mother had been able to keep the axe by bribing the guards. As was the case with the Jewish Holocaust in Germany, it was, by and large, those few who had money, social position and contacts who managed to escape, leaving the majority to suffer the worst fate. What follows is my account of the story told to Ahmed by his mother many times.

Umm Ahmed was born Sorbea Tatious Babezian. Her grandfather was a priest in eastern Turkey. Sorbea left her village, Esmet in Takerdag, with her aunt, mother and two sisters on an enforced 'three months' march'. She was fifteen. When it became clear that the march, described somewhat implausibly to them by the Turks as a work relocation, was in fact an extermination programme, Sorbea's aunt tattooed her niece's name in Armenian on her wrist. They were taken to Ezaz in northern Syria, where her mother, who collapsed from exhaustion, was killed, and then marched on to Meskene, which is where the mass killings started. After that they were driven like sheep along the Euphrates via Raqqa to Deir es Zor. Every day unspeakable things, the stuff of nightmares, were happening. The Chechnyan guards, employed by the Turks to do their dirty work, would take bets on the sex of the babies in the wombs of pregnant women and then rip them open to find out who had won. Mothers died by the wayside of starvation, heat stroke and exhaustion, often still attempting to breastfeed their malnourished infants, although their milk had long since dried up. Sorbea saw one dying woman hurl her baby into the Euphrates after her milk supply had given out and she could not stand the infant's agonized screams any longer. Women and girls were frequently raped as they were driven through the desert.

The deportees were kept alive with morsels of food handed to them by the Bedouins or the Syrian village people. The guards were unconcerned if they received a little sustenance to help them endure their torture for a few days more – they would all come to grief in the end. No one, walking naked in that sun and freezing in the desert at night, could last for long without contracting pneumonia or dysentery. A few lucky ones escaped at night, while others' children were purchased by the Bedouins from the venal guards. By the time she got to Deir, Sorbea's family had nothing left. As she was attractive and in better shape than most, she was swiftly married off to an Arab man.

Ironically, this was only the beginning of her problems. Sorbea's husband was already married. His first wife was jealous of the young Armenian girl, and resented the fact that she was persuading her husband to help her aunt and two sisters, who were in one of the camps full of dying Armenians strung along the riverbanks. She informed the Ottoman gendarmes, who at the time were organizing a mass march of the deportees back into the desert, to a lonely spot near Markada. Sorbea was rounded up once more and made to join them. At Markada the Turkish soldiers separated the men and boys from the women and children and proceeded to liquidate them. The men were bound together in groups of three or four and shot, a single bullet passing through the head of each member of the group. There was a sudden outbreak of disorder and random shooting broke out, killing Sorbea's aunt and two sisters, who had survived for so long against all the odds. Many others were herded together into nearby caves, where they were burned alive.

In the confusion, Sorbea managed to slip away. She ran until she finally found a peasant woman on a donkey. The woman helped her, and after a while they met a local gendarme who knew of Sorbea's husband. Together the gendarme and Sorbea rode on his horse to the Jier Dubat (pontoon bridge) at Al Hsanea, at that time the only way of crossing the Euphrates. There Sorbea was disguised as a boy. The soldier claimed that she was an employee of his brother's bakery on the other side of the river. Thus she was smuggled across, and taken to the soldier's sister's house until such time as she could be reunited with her husband.

Several years later her husband died, and she married a young Arab farmer. She continued to work as a tailor, a trade she had learned at her first husband's house, but moved to this village, where she spent the rest of her extraordinary long life, thanking God that she had been spared.

Ahmed brought out some photographs of his mother in her last years. She was an extremely impressive-looking woman with high cheekbones and a hooked nose, dressed in the style of the local country women in tiers of flowing patterned robes and a silk turban. I asked Ahmed whether it had ever occurred to his mother to convert back to Christianity. (On arrival in Deir, it was common practice for the girls to be converted, although many resisted this. Their religion was all they had left, and the one thing that for centuries had defined them as a separate race from their Turkish oppressors. Those of the girls for whom conversion was unthinkable tied their wrists together and jumped in groups into the Euphrates.) Ahmed replied that his mother always kept a Bible written in Armenian, which she would read as well as the Koran. 'Islam is good,' she had said. 'Christianity is good. But I prefer Islam because it is the religion of equality.' She had then quoted a sentence from the Koran: 'My faith is not acceptable if I do not help the poor and needy.'

As the story drew to an end (and it was a long time in the telling, as Tariq had to interpret), Ginny was showing signs of restlessness. 'Say, I'm really sorry to trouble you guys, but I gotta meet Dwight at the hotel by twelve-thirty. We're going on a trip with his class to Halabiya and Zalabiya.'

Now she tells us, I thought. It was already half past eleven. Tariq looked most concerned that his love was about to depart. Ahmed meanwhile said in Arabic that he had ordered two chickens to be slain in our honour, and that it would afford him great pleasure to give us lunch. 'I think Ahmed might be a little offended if you were to leave now,' I said to Ginny.

Probably imagining that Ginny was just being polite, Ahmed pressed her to stay, and a huge meal was carried in by the women of the household. 'You'll never get away now, darling,' I said.

'What am I going to do?' she wailed, standing up defiantly. 'Look, I'll pretend to go to the loo and then I can get my shoes on when I come back and then they'll know I mean business.'

She disappeared, returning some moments later. 'There isn't a loo,' she hissed.

'You just have to go out and squat in the bushes behind the house,' I replied, noticing that she had relocated her shoes, thus proclaiming her firm intention to leave and reunite herself with Dwight. I told Tariq to make it clear that Ginny was utterly consumed with sorrow and embarrassment at having to leave early, but that it was all prearranged and there was simply not a thing she could do to get out of it. A boy was sent on his bike to the village, and eventually a battered little trezeena spluttered up the track to the farm and Ginny was borne away to her tryst in a style to which she was not accustomed.

Hours later, utterly worn out with hospitality, Tariq and I also left. I too had to pay a visit to the shrubbery. It was a little grove studded with wizened turds about which one had to tiptoe looking for a little corner that one felt could accommodate one's needs. Once ensconced, however, there was a lovely view over the countryside. Somewhere tactfully in the distance, one of Ahmed's sons hovered with a pitcher of water in one hand and a bar of olive oil soap in the other.

When it was our turn to get into the trezeena, we bumped not only along the track through the fields but all the way back into town along the main road, crossing the modern bridge over the Euphrates. Was it my imagination, or was I really the subject of curiosity and no little mirth, a tall, linen-suited *ajnabee* sitting in the front of this lowly conveyance, being forced into the gutter by passing lorries as we farted along at fifteen kilometres per hour?

Tariq was stretched out in the trailer at the back. When we arrived he planted a huge wadge of freshly made bread from the farmer's oven into my arms. 'They said to be sure to give this to Ginny as she missed her lunch,' he said.

'Sure,' I replied, making a mental note: bread to Ginny, bones to Aleppo.

27

A Ring of Silver

My last trip with Tariq and Ginny was to Shaddadeh. He was very keen that I should see the cave between Deir es Zor and Hasseke where over eighty thousand Armenians had been exterminated in one of the most appalling crimes of the massacre.

It was an ugly village several kilometres off the main road. We managed to hire a pick-up to take us up into the fertile terrain behind it, crossing the Khabour river on the way. The driver knew Shaddadeh, and took us as far as his car would allow. We walked the rest of the way, scrambling up a shale bank on which a large water-refining tank had been placed. From here we could see for miles over the surrounding irrigated cornfields, but immediately around us was dry, barren stone, white in the glare of the heat. We split up and looked for the opening of the cave, which took far longer than expected. (It was forbidden to indicate the whereabouts of the cave with any form of public sign.) Tariq had told us that this was a place of pilgrimage for Armenians the world over – they came every year on the official anniversary of the outbreak of the massacre, from Paris, Los Angeles, Lebanon, Cyprus and Beirut, to light candles in memory of the dead which they embedded in the soft soil of the cave floor.

After about forty minutes I heard a cry and saw Tariq waving to me in the distance. I walked over to him. He was standing on the edge of a large triangular cleft plunging directly into the ground. We clambered down a drop of about ten feet and entered an extensive but shallow cave. It was remarkably cool compared to the raging heat outside. To our right I noticed a bank of maidenhair fern, startling in its greenness – a gash of colour and life against the dead black rock. We were tired and hot, so we sat down for a while to rest.

Shaddadeh was rumoured to be an almost endless cave – some of the Bedouins said that it was roughly fifty kilometres long, but this may have been a colourful exaggeration. The story was that the column of deportees was marched to this lonely spot and some were forced to stumble one by one into the cave. Once inside they were burned alive. Others were shot and left outside to decompose, their bodies picked clean by the jackals and desert wolves. When the rains came their bones were swept into the cave and were eventually washed into the river beyond. Umm Ahmed's son had told me that he had seen bones floating down the river near his house.

We walked further into the cave. The ground beneath our feet was extremely uneven, wet and muddy. We could touch the roof. I tried to imagine what it must have been like for the tragic, brutalized souls who had met their end here. It would only have taken one person to stumble and fall in the panic that would inevitably have ensued when the smoke and flames began to lick around the cave to create a huge pile-up of bodies. Very few would have been able to move. Eighty thousand was a staggering number of human beings to kill in one go, and with such an inefficient and slow method.

The only lighting material we had with us was an old newspaper and a box of matches, and very soon we had used the paper up. Looking behind us, we could see a dim light from the mouth of the cave. It was said that the young and able scrambled ahead of the others, and that one young boy managed to climb out of the cave before the poisonous fumes got to him at a place where it joined the river, and was thus able to alert the local villagers to what had happened. Today there is no trace of the appalling massacre – just a series of caves that any schoolboy would love to explore, and a bank of maidenhair fern. But even to this day the name Shaddadeh retains its resonance, striking horror into every Armenian's soul.

We had arranged for the driver to return and collect us at three o'clock. On the way back, instead of returning to the road, he took a short cut over the desert, and it was not long before we came to grief on the rocks. We all had to alight and try to heave the pick-up out of a ditch. All our efforts would not budge it. Ginny was, as usual, on her way to meet Dwight. It was her birthday and an appropriately celebratory event had been planned. Eventually a peasant trotted by on a donkey, and his brawny strength combined with our effete attempts finally got us back into action. We bounced off towards the road and were deposited by the junction to await the next bus.

Back in Deir es Zor we stopped a passing cab so that Ginny could complete the final leg of her relay to reunion with Dwight. We said our fond farewells, as I was leaving the next day. 'If you want me, just dial me up,' she said, making herself sound like a pizza and planting a kiss on each of my cheeks. She looked uncertainly at Tariq, who leaped forward and planted a lingering kiss on both of hers. Ginny kissed the air next to his face. 'Goodbye, Tariq. Thanks for everything,' she said, slumping into the back of the taxi.

When we got back to Tariq's house he upbraided me for having let Ginny travel on her own in the taxi. 'We must phone the hotel now. We must!' he cried. 'It is not safe for a tourist to travel on her own in a taxi. Recently a blond-haired tourist was taken back to the taximan's home and raped!'

'Poor girl,' I said. 'I hope they punished her attackers severely.'

Tariq looked at me. 'It was a man,' he said, awkwardly.

That last night Tariq was very glum. We went back to his house, and he occupied himself writing a letter in English, drawing extensively on his Arabic/English dictionary. Occasionally he would look up and ask, 'How do you spell "longing"?' or 'If I gave Ginny a silver ring as a leaving present, would it be appropriate?' To this I cruelly replied that it would not really be appropriate as men only gave women rings when they were romantically attached to them.

Before I went back to the Raghdan, Tariq asked me to meet him at his friend's shop the next day before my bus left, so that he could hand over the box of bones. Unfortunately I missed the appointment, so I went to his house. His sister answered the door, and I told her in my limited Arabic that I would be catching the eleven o'clock bus that morning.

While waiting for the bus to arrive, I went into a little parfumier's, and to my delight discovered that they sold carnation oil. This oil is used only medicinally in the Arab world, and they find it very strange that anyone should want to use it as a perfume. I had two bottles of eau-de-Cologne made up, asking the parfumier to mix two parts carnation with one part clove. There was a cabinet in the shop full of old perfume bottles from Dior, St Laurent, Armani and many other famous names. They were somewhat the worse for wear, but I liked the idea of recycling these beautiful objects. The parfumier filled them with a solution of fixative, alcohol and oil and attached new plastic nozzles to the spraying devices, finally resealing them with a little copper band around the rim.

As I was leaving the shop to catch the bus, Tariq bounded up to me. 'I am very sorry, Robert,' he said. 'I went to the hotel when you did not come to the shop, but they told me you had already left.' This was a blatant lie on the part of the hotel staff as I had not checked out until after I had returned from my botched appointment. Clearly they did not wish to encourage any contact between me and the native Syrians.

'Where's the box?' I asked.

'I took it back to the church. I thought you had gone and I had missed you.'

'Never mind,' I said. I was in truth relieved to be discharged of my strange duty.

'Please, Robert. Take this with you and post it when you get to London.'

Tariq handed me a letter, addressed to Ginny. I boarded the bus and he stood on the kerb waving until it had left.

Months later in London, when I was clearing out my rucksack, I turned up the letter again, secreted in one of its remoter pockets. I had forgotten all about my commission. The envelope had come unstuck, so I took the letter out.

Dear Ginny (it read)

I hope you receive this letter and you are well. I phoned in Wednesday night at 10.30 in the evening to the Hotel Ferat Cham but the official there told me you (all) had gone. Excuse me I could not to phone at 10 o'clock as we agree at Shaddadeh village, because I had two guests Robert and my friend Aziz. Excuse me again because perhaps you have been waiting by the phone for an hour in vain.

I phoned again at 10 o'clock in the morning (Thursday) but I was told that you have left (Deir es Zor). So I was so sad, because I wanted to see you and to present you with a gift. A ring of silver with a red bead.

I want to tell you that which I was not brave enough to say: I loved you. Perhaps you do not feel this emotion with me (but I can love you from one side). Because Love sometimes is from one side. I am longing to see you again.

I was admired with your kind speech and I was admired with you because you did not hurt me although I was curious with you and I asked you a lot of questions. Please forgive me if I mistook to you in any thing. And I want to say again I loved you from all my heart. And I will not love beside you (another girl, I mean). For the rest of my life. I hope you will visit me as you promised. I am waiting for you.

My best regards to your parents and your brothers and sisters.

Tariq

Lady Anne Blunt, who travelled in Syria in the nineteenth century, was right when she observed that with the Arabs a little goes a long way. I folded the letter up again, feeling a pinprick of guilt.

28

So, Why?

Back at the Rose, I had received a letter from a friend in England
with an introduction to the English owner of the Baron Hotel, Mrs
Maslumian. We sat in the dining room having lunch at the very table
I had seen F waddle off to on my first day in Syria.

Sally Maslumian had, the day before, celebrated her forty-ninth
year in Syria. She had met and married her Armenian husband Coco
when she was nursing in Aleppo after the war. She had come to Syria
as a result of knowing a family from Coniston in the Lake District.
The father was an Armenian doctor who had married an English wife
and they had had five children. They travelled between Aleppo
(where the doctor had a hospital in Suleymania) and England, where
their next-door neighbour was Arthur Ransome. The five half-
Syrian, half-English children were to be the inspiration for his most
famous book, *Swallows and Amazons*.

I found it a strange experience talking to her, rather like talking
to an English person through a glass screen. To all intents and
purposes she looked and sounded English, but at the same time she
had become something else. She referred to the Armenians as 'we'
and Armenia as the 'occupied territories'. 'Occupied since the tenth
century,' said her half-English, half-Armenian son Armen languidly
in his faintly accented English, pulling on his pipe.

The lunch was a splendid affair, consisting of Syrian mezze,
artichokes and rice and then good old roast potatoes and gravy.
There was fresh fruit and coffee to follow. Mrs Maslumian said that
she did not miss England. 'Only the green. And sometimes Christ-
mas. But I've been here so long I've forgotten what I used to miss.'

She was not the most forthcoming of conversationalists, perhaps
because she had acquired a dislike of writers and journalists. Twice
she and the hotel had been written about in books in a light that she
thought unrepresentational, if not treacherous. 'As for journalists,

they always tell you that they'll send you a copy of what they've written and of course they never do,' she remarked wryly.

'On the subject of journalists, I don't suppose you remember F, do you?' I asked, adding: 'I met him here a few months ago.'

Mrs Maslumian rolled her eyes and said, 'Oh, F.' She turned to her son, who was gazing abstractedly into the bar, and asked him, 'Did you hear that, Armen? He knows F.'

'Oh dear me,' commented Armen, and he and his mother exchanged glances.

'He was drunk most of the time,' continued Mrs Maslumian. 'He was completely drunk when he interviewed us in my son's office and, for some strange reason, he insisted on bringing a young Dane with him. He wanted to take my photograph. I said, "Why? Firstly, I'm not photogenic, secondly I *hate* having my photograph taken, and thirdly they'll never come out." About six weeks later I got a letter from him from England. It said that he could not send me the article he had written for the *Evening Standard* as he'd handed it to the secretary who unfortunately had mislaid it. As for the photographs, he explained that none of them had come out because he had omitted to take the cap off the lens. I could have told him that anyway.'

'The Dane was very strange,' added Armen in his slow, lugubrious tones. 'He was convinced I was into numismatics because F had told him so, and every time he saw me afterwards – which was always at a difficult time – he demanded, "Show me your mints," as he kept calling them. He came to the bar with some very strange people.'

I could not leave the Baron without asking Mrs Maslumian for her reminiscences of Agatha Christie, who wrote the first part of *Murder on the Orient Express* in the hotel.

'My husband met the Mallowans in the dining room one evening. He had a bad habit of saying, instead of "Come for supper," "Come for a drink." He also had a bad habit of being in the bath when the guests arrived. On the day I prepared dinner for the Mallowans my sister rang. She was a great fan, so I included her and her English husband as well as the consul for Isakanderun and his wife whom I had already invited. Then my husband thought it would be better to make the dinner party into a buffet and invite a few more people, and so the whole thing grew.

'At six the Mallowans arrived expecting to stay for one hour for drinks. I opened the door and in waddled Agatha Christie – and I mean waddled, for her legs were absolutely huge, each one like this.'

(She marked off half the width of the dining table to illustrate her point.) 'She saw the other people and sat glumly on the sofa. I took great care to introduce her very correctly as Mrs Mallowan, and took the cigarettes round in the silver box we kept them in. (You always did this if you had a difficult guest while you were thinking. I remember thinking she was a complete pill.) Then I asked her what she would like to drink. "Nothing, thank you," she replied.

'Not even an orange or tomato juice?' I asked. In the end she agreed to have a tomato juice, and then my sister came along and I was very happy to pass her on to her.

'I went to the kitchen to see how dinner was coming along and returned to say, "Dinner is served." Just as I was saying it I heard the consul proclaiming, in a rather loud voice, "And *my* name's Napoleon." One of the other guests had told him that this large silent woman on the sofa was Agatha Christie. He bounded across the room and cried, "But why is it that I had no idea that the wonderful Agatha Christie was going to be with us tonight!" He was, needless to say, a great fan of hers.

'After this outburst, Mrs Mallowan changed completely towards us. You see, she imagined I had rung around town and said, "Guess what, I've got Agatha Christie coming to dinner tonight" and got a whole group of fans together. When she realized that no one, apart from me and my sister, knew who she was, she relaxed. I remember particularly her joining in the conversation over dinner about lipstick. In those days they had just developed the new replaceable type of lipstick which meant you didn't have to buy the old sort which came in a silver box and was very expensive. She was fascinated to know how you inserted the new lipstick into the compact. After this she stayed in the hotel often.'

The conversation moved on to the trains and Aleppo railway station. 'It didn't have those awful chandeliers before,' said Mrs Maslumian, 'or those ideological paintings. The train was always known as the Orient Express, though technically after Istanbul it was the Istanbul Express.'

Armen added, 'The train centre of Syria is Aleppo, which is the only thing Aleppo excels in over Damascus. But Damascus is a dead end. There are no trains beyond Damascus.' He lapsed back into puffing on his pipe, searching through the pockets of his baggy tweed jacket for his tobacco.

I was reflecting that it must have been a strange life for Mrs

Maslumian during the years of the Cold War as an émigrée in a
pariah state with very few compatriots around her. 'We have been in
the doghouse a few times,' she agreed. 'The first time was during
Suez when there were no diplomatic relations between England and
Syria. The second was after 1967.'

Armen explained how the Arab countries were given a face-saving
device after the humiliating 1967 defeat. 'They said that America and
England had provided Israel with air power for the war.' Relations
were severed again, and the effect on the part-English-run Baron was
obvious. 'It turned out,' continued Armen, 'that this theory was all
nonsense as Mossad came up with a taped conversation they had
intercepted between Nasser and King Hussein of Jordan agreeing on
this plan in order to save face. Relations between Syria and England
were eventually restored.' Restored, that is, until the infamous
Hindawi affair. 'In 1983 we lost them again,' continued Armen,
'when the pregnant Irish woman boarded an El Al plane carrying a
bomb which she was unaware of. It had been planted by her lover,
who was a Palestinian. The problem was he had entered Britain on
a Syrian visa. The security official at the Syrian embassy was called
in for questioning, but Syria refused to lift diplomatic immunity.
Relations were restored again in the early nineties as a prize for Syria
taking the right side in the Gulf War.' And so the seesaw of international interests continued.

Despite her wariness towards journalists, Mrs Maslumian was a
very good raconteur. She kept a completely straight face when telling
me her stories – I do not recall seeing her smile once. The only time
she betrayed any emotion was when I said I wanted to write something about the Armenian massacres. In some ways she reminded me
of Gunde, the German lady married to a Palestinian. Both of them
had traded their loyalties and to some extent their identities for that
of their new race acquired through marriage (one could not say their
new country, as both Palestine and Armenia have been virtually
eradicated as sovereign territories). It was probably the only way to
survive the cultural leap that led them both to become members of
minority races, their lives henceforth locked into the other side of
the ideological and political divide. Theirs were lives lived, in effect,
behind the Arab – Soviet Iron Curtain.

After lunch I noticed on the wall of the hotel, under the terrace,
a tiny orange kitten sleeping in the hot sun only yards from the busy
traffic. I popped into Rachid's tourist shop and told him about it. He

was talking to a strange fellow in striped trousers which made him look like a clown; he had a weaselly, sinister face. He was a Jordanian, and told me that it was his job to excavate Byzantine and Roman mosaics, glassware and jewellery illegally and flog them on the black market. This he claimed to do with the assistance of a highly placed Baath Party official who lived in Lattakia. He said that he had just furnished him with two fantastic mosaics of classical scenes. 'In this country you can only get six thousand dollars each for them. The main thing is to get them to Europe.' I asked him how this was done. 'There is only one way,' he replied. 'That is through the diplomatic luggage.' I drew him out on the subject and he promised to take me to meet the person concerned so that I could look at the mosaics, which he hoped I could help sell through my contacts in London's more prestigious auction houses. (This happened to me several times. I would be spirited off to the flat of some friend of a friend of a friend and confronted with an Old Master and asked to pronounce on its authenticity and market value. Once it turned out that the painting in question had been stolen from the King of Morocco.)

When I mentioned the kitten on the wall, the shady art smuggler said he knew exactly what to do. He took me to see his friend who ran a hardware store near the souk. He was a sweet fellow who had two long-haired cats which, when we arrived, were sleeping in the shop window, sunning themselves in the plastic bowls he sold. Every night this man drove his car around the back streets of Aleppo, putting down food for the local stray cats. He reckoned to feed approximately 150 cats a day. He disappeared upstairs and returned minutes later with a large bowl full of fresh offal. It was covered with an old glasscloth and resting on the top was a large block of ice to keep it cool. The shopkeeper said he had three such bowls, and that when he drove around all the cats ran out to wait for him as they had learned to recognize the sound of his engine. He said that everyone he knew thought he was mad, but that this did not bother him unduly as he was performing this charity for the love not only of cats but of Allah. He spent over twelve dollars a day on the cat food, and one day he would receive his reward in heaven, if Allah so willed it.

I asked the shopkeeper if I could accompany him on his feeding mission one evening, and he said it would give him great pleasure if I would do so; he suggested I return that evening at eight. When I did return a few minutes after eight, however, I found the shop locked up. The next day I went into the shop, fondled the cats and was invited to sit down and take tea by the shopkeeper, who seemed as amiable as ever. Then he turned to me and said with a hurt look, 'Where were you last night?' I told him that I had arrived as agreed, if a few minutes late, and that I would still like to go with him one night on his cat-feeding mission. He said that it would be difficult that night as he had a business meeting, but the day after would be fine.

The next day I returned at the suggested time. I was with a French student whom I had originally met in Bosra, who had turned up at the hotel. The shopkeeper was sitting with a circle of friends taking tea, smoking and talking. He said that he would be free in about an hour. The Frenchman and I wandered off and returned about forty minutes later and waited outside the shop as the owner was still inside talking. All around us was the nerve-racking sound of aluminium shutters being pulled down and padlocked. Suddenly I heard the distinctive noise of the shopkeeper's old Oldsmobile as it pulled away from its parking space near the shop, and saw it slip into a stream of traffic heading for the citadel. I found it most strange that the shopkeeper had not seen me standing only yards away from his shop and within feet of his car.

I decided to go back one last time the next day. The shopkeeper again was friendly, and professed his distress at my not turning up the night before. 'But I did turn up,' I managed to convey in my faltering Arabic. 'I was outside your shop with my French friend at the time agreed.' The shopkeeper shrugged and said that if that was the case he certainly had not seen me. I replied that I would still dearly love to accompany him on his mercy mission, and he informed me that that would be fine but it would have to be in a week's time as he was going away on business. The next day, however, his shop was open and he was sitting in it, taking tea with his friends as usual.

I could not for the life of me understand what was going on. Why was the shopkeeper so friendly? Why did he constantly renew his invitation and then engineer things so that I was excluded from his plans? I decided to ask Rachid the next time I saw him.

Rachid looked at me keenly when I posed the question. He cleared his throat portentously and said, 'You remember the man who introduced you to the shopkeeper?' I said I did. 'Well, this is nothing to do with me, you understand. But for many years this man lived in America and it is his opinion that you are a homosexual. The shopkeeper also appears to think this is the case. Perhaps this is something to do with it.'

'I see,' I said. 'On what basis has he formed this opinion?' I hardly needed to ask.

'He said you were wearing an earring.'

'Whether I was wearing an earring or not,' I retorted, 'does not entitle him to keep inviting me round to his shop when he's not there, when he has no intention of keeping his arrangement with me.'

'But this is typical Arabic behaviour,' replied Rachid. 'Perhaps the shopkeeper did not wish to cause you offence. It is the same all the time here. How many times are my parents just about to go out? They are dressed to go out and the doorbell rings and some friends arrive. My mother cannot turn them away. It is impossible, even though it is obvious they are about to go out. She has to make them tea and sometimes she even phones the people she originally had to meet with an excuse and puts off the arrangement until another time.'

I had heard before that an Arab would rather stand you up than say no to your face, but this seemed to be taking things a little far. It was a small incident but it shook the foundations of my experiences in Syria. How much of the hospitality and friendliness I had received over the last few months had been extended on a similar basis? Perhaps all I had been doing all along was pressing the hospitality button. But surely not with Jihad, with Tadeus?

Tariq had warned me against Tadeus. 'Do not tell him about any of your experiences,' he had said. 'Do not tell him about going to Shaddadeh or to the Roman tombs to collect the bones. I think he is Mukhabarat. He asked me many questions on the phone. His English is too good.' I just did not understand the situation, and the more I thought about it the more I doubted that I ever would.

29

A Letter on Grey Paper

For several weeks I had been feeling tired all the time, although I had assumed that I had more or less recovered from my first illness. When I look at my diary, the entries for the last few weeks I spent in Syria are full of references to feeling increasingly exhausted, depressed and weak, in between recording a fairly hectic schedule in temperatures over 40°C. My stomach upset had returned. Rachid told me that I was looking very ill. 'You are very thin now, and your skin has lost its elasticity. You must have a rehydration therapy.' He wrote down the name of a medication used by UNESCO and I bought some from a nearby chemist. On the way home that night I met a German tourist whom I had come across occasionally on my travels. 'If your diarrhoea has blood in it, it is typhus. If the blood is black it is a bleeding stomach ulcer, but if it is only water then it is cholera. If it's none of these things it is just an ordinary stomach upset,' he said comfortingly. I had not previously thought of my illness in any of these terms. I hoped he was either an alarmist or just trying to be funny.

Groggily, I went to bed, vaguely aware of impending horror. Somewhere way below, as I fell asleep, the great printing presses were stamping impatiently, relentlessly. Several hours later, in the middle of the night, I awoke, but now the pounding was firmly inside my head. I had been dreaming of standing in a forest, looking up at the gaps of white sky between the leaves. The pattern of white and green was driving me insane. I was lying in a pool of sweat that had soaked into the bedsheets. Every bone and joint was aching and I had a very high fever.

The next morning the fever had abated somewhat. As I lay prone, watching the revolutions of the wobbly, off-centre ceiling fan, wondering if it would fly off and decapitate me, Abdulkabir came to see me and took my temperature. It was now a staggering 41°C. I was so hot that several veins had burst in my face. He told me to wear a wet towel like a turban that night, and to drape more wet towels over my body. I also had to shower my head, feet and legs regularly to keep my temperature down.

Another day of fluctuating temperature followed in which I lay on the bed drifting in and out of consciousness. Abdulkabir kept calling in to see me, with Tadeus or Baby Shoes or Rachid or whoever was passing. At one point I woke up to find Karim sitting on the bed opposite, looking very beautiful and solemn. His thick black glossy fringe was hanging shaggily over one eye. We exchanged a few words, and Karim said he had heard I was here from Abdulkabir, whom he had met in the street. He had to see Rupert, he said, and he wanted me to help him go to England. I told him that in that case he would have to get an invitation from Rupert. 'Where is Rupert?' I asked. 'How is he?' Karim said he thought he was in England but that he had not heard from him. He pulled a letter out of his shirt pocket and gave it to me with just one word: 'Please.' I took it and nodded, and Karim held out his hand. As we shook hands he kissed me elaborately, once on one cheek, twice on the other and finally on my right shoulder. He looked at me gently but unsmilingly and walked out of the room. I noticed that he was wearing a gun in a holster strapped round his waist. It was an air pistol. One day soon it would be a real one.

I looked at the envelope, on which Rupert's name and address were written clearly if childishly. The notepaper inside was visible through the cheap thin material. I could see that it was graph paper, which everyone seemed to use in Syria. I wondered where Rupert was now, and what would happen to his friendship with Karim. Perhaps it had ended already. That was what happened with these sorts of relationships: they finished at a moment that passed without your knowing it. Then came the letters, the difficult, expensive phone calls, the bungled invitations, the failed visa applications, and after a few months you realized what you should have appreciated weeks before. It was over. Your efforts to revive it were like blowing air into the lungs of a corpse.

After an hour or two of lying in misery on my bed, the temptation was too much. When I had visitors I was distracted for a while, but on my own I felt very conscious of my suffering. By opening the letter I would have another sort of visit, and I am sure that Rupert would have understood. I called the Kurdish boy, Nazmi, and asked him to steam the letter open with the kettle in reception. It came back soggy but intact.

In the Name of God (it read at the top)

My friend Mr Rupert
I write to you with my respects and my love from Syria. Are you back in your beautiful country nowadays? Have you many beautiful memories of our time together in Syria this summer and last summer? I think about you every day with great love in my heart.

I am write to you to say if you come here again I promise you one million of welcomes. I will take you to the river at Midanky to swim together in the waterfal. We can take orangez and opples and bananas and drink mulberry juice and make kebabs. And we can take the bus to Nebi Houri on the roman bridge. And we can listen to Assalla Nassri on my Walkman. You remember the song, you like very much: Walad Sada – wretched boy?

I will sing to you your favourite Lebanese song and play the drums. I will do everything I can to make you happy with me.

I am sorry. I am sorry. I am one thousand times sorry. Please forgive me. Please.

Mr Rupert. You say you can take me to England to see London and the Queen's Palce. And see the park and lakes. Enclose is my passport number and address. And please instead of trainers can I have leather boots. And a cap with BOY on the front.

I wait to hear from you everyday. You are in my eyes and heart and I kiss your face from far away.

My regards to your family.
Karim
I love you. I miss you.

I put the letter down, reflecting on its mixture of emotion and materialism, and wished I had not read it. It had obviously been written by a friend. Reading between the lines, it looked as though something had gone very wrong between them.

All the people who came to see me joked extensively and tried to cheer me up and then had prolonged conversations with Abdulkabir in subdued Arabic. That night Abdulkabir told me that he thought I had classic typhoid symptoms and that I would have to go to hospital for a blood test. I was so shocked I felt as if someone had administered a blow to my stomach.

By now I had eaten virtually nothing for two days, and the biting pains I had experienced several weeks before were returning in my lower gut. The newspapers that week were full of the terrible cockroach plague that had hit Aleppo, and every night Nazmi came to my room and splattered the biggest ones he could find or shot at them with a jet of insecticide in a squeedgy can.

One young man staying in the hotel was a student from Deir es Zor. I asked him what had happened to the lake of oil that had been building up there. He told me that in the end static electricity from someone's clothes had set it alight and that five people – two Americans, two Malaysians and one Syrian – had been killed in the blast. Their bodies would never be recovered. The explosion had caused a fire with temperatures that reached 500°C.

Abdulkabir came early the next day. I was feeling like death. We took a taxi to see his cousin, a haematologist in a local hospital. It was a thoroughly depressing experience for someone with a boiling temperature. Tadeus had told me that normally a trip to this hospital was something to be avoided, but since I was European and had a connection with the haematologist he would probably 'take special care to do the test properly'. (Normally, he explained, they took too long between each stage of the test, or went off for a cup of tea and forgot to time it, thus invalidating the results.)

The haematologist had trained in Bucharest. He looked considerably cleaner than the hospital, which had old handkerchiefs and litter lining the corridors, while the staircases were encrusted with filth. In the haematology departments the employees were sitting around smoking; people were also smoking in the corridors. A woman in a veil was lying in agony on her side on a trolley with no sheets on it in the corridor, her eyes open and glazed with pain. Bedouins wearing red-and-white keffiyehs were squatting on their haunches, smoking, outside the door.

The haematologist, I noticed with relief, used a sterilized needle, but after mopping up some blood which had trickled down my arm (he wasn't wearing protective gloves) he flicked the soiled cotton wool swab through an open window. He offered me some chilled water in a glass, and then he and his colleagues swigged, Arab style, from the same bottle. I sat in a daze waiting for the result to come through. Suddenly a great ululation went up from a group of women in another part of the building: someone had died in the ward down the corridor. I wondered whether, if my result turned out to be positive, I should not book them for me too, just in case.

A few minutes later the haematologist rushed back into the room, looking very pleased with himself and rather excited. The test had proved to be positive: I had one strain of typhoid and one of paratyphoid. It was impossible to tell where or how I had picked them up, whether from a sewage-polluted water supply or through food prepared by hands carrying traces of faeces.

A doctor was summoned to look at the result, but she said it could not be typhoid as I had not been ill for long enough. When I explained that I had previously been ill with a bad stomach disorder, however, this was deemed to be the first phase of the disease – typhoid is apparently biphasal. I insisted on another test. Abdulkabir suggested an Armenian doctor whose claim to fame was that he had witnessed an operation on George Bush's leg as a medical student in the US. There were no taxis to be had outside the hospital and by then it was midday and the temperature was 43°C (only three degrees above my own). We waited for what seemed an age while I found a wall to lean against, clutching my tummy and yearning for Blighty.

We arrived near the surgery in a hellishly crowded minibus and then walked for five minutes through the merciless heat. I was given a clearly superior and more thorough blood test, and the result was indeed positive (though this one claimed I had both strains of typhoid and neither of paratyphoid).

Fortunately, I had taken out a travel insurance policy. Strangely, rather than transporting me to a private hospital where there might have been food and nurses, the insurance company booked me into a five-star hotel. I later received a bolshy message from them saying that they had no intention of paying for any food I might require. So soon I found myself with typhoid in an expensive five-star hotel, faced with paying for food that was well beyond my humble budget.

When I arrived at the Amir Palace, my baggage carried by Nazmi, my room had not been prepared. I was asked to sit in the lobby by the bookshop and partake of a 'welcome drink'. The whole situation seemed so inappropriate to one in my plight. Muzak was oozing out of some concealed speakers, and everyone looked more Westernized than the cast of *Dynasty*. I was in the homogenized world of the five-star hotel, that international dollar culture of muzak, lobbies and welcome drinks.

The doctor (erroneously, it now seems) told me that I could eat anything, apart from milk. I later learned that the pinching pains I could feel were actually the lower gut ulcerating, and that the wrong sort of food could pierce these ulcers and cause peritonitis. At that moment, however, ignorance was bliss. An obliging waiter appeared and unobligingly told me that I would have to pay for room service in US dollars. I had long since run out of these and was now using my remaining traveller's cheques. There was only one alternative: I was forced to eat meals at the self-service buffet in the hotel restaurant, thus turning myself into the Typhoid Mary of Aleppo. Looking back, I think it extremely unlikely that the insurance company had told the hotel that they were imposing a typhoid victim on them.

As I entered my room, I noticed a paper seal around the mouthpiece of the telephone, on which was written 'This telephone has been sterilized for your protection', a fact I found rather ironic considering that I was one giant ambulant virus at the time. From my window I had a fine view of the citadel and the minaret of the Great Mosque. The whole of Aleppo was out there at my feet, but I didn't want it any more. The double glazing meant that the polluted, rackety din of the town came to me as from a remote world with which I had severed all connection save the visual one. I was looking at life as a phobic might, through a cinema screen in a private auditorium with the sound turned very low. The constant blare of car horns, which had been driving me mad, was now no more distracting than the squeaking of a hamster. The nerve-racking rattle and screech of the shop shutters, which previously had driven me almost to insanity, was forever silenced. The hammering of cobblers' awls and the frivolous trill of their frustrated, imprisoned canaries were no more. I did not miss any of it. I never wanted to go out into that heat, dust, noise, pollution and chaos again. I wanted to retreat into my germicidal bubble for ever.

I caught a glimpse of myself in the full-length mirror – the first I had had since my illness set in, the first probably for weeks. I was transfixed by this vision of myself with something like appalled horror. I peeled off my clothes to get into the shower. All the flesh was hanging off my body so that I looked like a chapati.

I spent the next five days in the hotel, watching the loop of news on CNN all day. Every so often – relief of reliefs – they would squeeze another item into the loop. An American artist had painted an entire landscape in oils on the side of a grain of rice; a prostitute had given Hugh Grant a blowjob on Sunset Boulevard. Nice to be in touch again. From my secluded little sanatorium in the air, life in the West did not look particularly pleasant.

By this time I was suffering from the most appalling flatulence, and for a while I thought that my end would come not from typhoid but rather from methane asphyxiation. I used to pray that no one would visit during these horrifying paroxysms, but usually managed to stagger to the door and hang the 'Do not disturb' sign on the handle when I fell under their awful tyranny.

One day Abdulkabir came to see me looking agitated. Kamal had disappeared, no one knew where to. A neighbour had seen him getting into a car and no one had heard from him since. His wife had gone to the police station – the beautiful old Ottoman one in Azizieh – where she took her place in the crowd milling outside, a crowd of mothers, brothers, fathers and sisters of those who went missing from the streets every day. I used to see them every night when I walked back to the hotel from Tadeus's house – a forlorn knot of people on the opposite corner, standing in the dark, white-faced with anxiety, motionless as skittles, all mournfully facing in the same direction, waiting for some indication of when their loved ones might be released.

'Strange,' I said. 'I always thought Kamal was Mukhabarat anyway.'

'People are saying,' responded Abdulkabir, 'that he was Mukhabarat, but also working for the Kurds as well.'

So that was it, I thought. Kamal had been a double agent flogging titbits to the Mukhabarat as a cover while at the same time running a cell connected to some banned Kurdish group. I suddenly felt horrified on his behalf.

'They went to his house. Found some papers ...' Abdulkabir shrugged and looked sad. His voice trailed off into silence – the silence that enclosed the forbidden realms of conversation.

After a week I managed to stagger out of the hotel and buy a ticket home. I was not getting any better. I was depressed, lonely and gradually losing control. The time, as it always must, had come to leave. You always recognize it when it comes, and I welcomed it with open arms.

It was Rachid's father who gave me a lift to the airport. I liked him, with his wired-up front teeth and very badly dyed hair, carroty-red with a good inch of grey at the roots. He had some good news for Rachid. As an ex-officer it was his prerogative to choose where his son could do his national service. He was hoping that he could arrange for him to serve in Aleppo, and he was going to break the news to him that night. I regarded him in a new light after this. He did not look at all how I had imagined a Syrian officer would look.

I remember watching the trees lining the roads, and all along the grass islands in the middle the poor, from the blocks with no gardens or balconies, eating their picnics, glad to escape the heat of their boxed existence for a while. They reminded me of the shepherd boys sleeping on the pavements of Damascus. They would stay there until well after darkness fell, whole families plumped on traffic islands, dusty verges, roundabouts, food spread out around them, beneath the stunted, dust-coated trees, every bite they took laced with poison.

At the airport I spent the rest of my Syrian money and started to go through the formalities. On one wall was a sign reading: 'All non-Syrians are kindly requested to keep their entry cards with them at all times. Without them they cannot enter or depart the cuntry [sic].' You said it, I thought, before hobbling through the checkpoint. A woman with long peroxide-blond hair and bright pink nail varnish checked me in. Behind her on the wall was a positive gallery of Basseliana: Bassel on a horse, Bassel with his father in fatigues, Bassel floating in the heavens, smiling down over a view of the citadel of Aleppo, where Karim had leaned nonchalantly the day I first saw him playing his pipe.

When I got through to the other side I was feeling very unsteady and I collapsed onto a plastic chair, my head reeling. All of it – the fear, the paranoia, the discovery and excitement, the love, longing, separation, pain, beauty and ugliness – was swirling round and round like a kaleidoscope in my palsied brain. If travel is like life, then it was only apt that the end should have come as it did. The bugle had finally sounded. I was beating a retreat.

Epilogue

For a whole month I languished in bed in England. One day I received a letter from Rupert, postmarked Hong Kong. After the usual politenesses I came to an intriguing section.

I left Syria [he wrote] in some considerable distress. I was a fool to go back like that, but I cannot regret it. You must follow your heart. I now see – I knew before it started – it was an utterly hopeless and ridiculous situation. I loved (love) Karim and I make allowances for his deprived situation. But I could not bear the fact that after I left for Jordan – who knows, even before – he had started an affair with George. He was always overimpressed with G. Always mentioning him, going to see him. Those stories of his stealing things were all a lie, a cover, sham, whatever. And I feel I shall hate George for ever. He is a pure hypocrite. In public always attacking Karim, sneering at him, saying he was dishonest, a thief. Nothing as dishonest as seducing a young boy with material things for sexual favours and then covering it up with lies.

Karim, I am sure, did not love him. On the other hand, I am not sure that he loved me, though he always said he did and I am experienced enough to know the difference between passion and lust, sexual opportunism and tenderness. I feel so destroyed. Such a damn fool.

I have resolved to leave England. Is it too awful to lead a life of sexual exile? Is that what I am doing? I am on my way to Indonesia, where a friend of mine is teaching English. I am going to have a recce on the work front myself. They say it is totally unspoiled – like Syria, like Karim (Oh God). You must come out and join me. Address overleaf ...

The letter explained a lot. It all added up – the Walkman, George's victimization of Karim, his lust fuelling his hatred of him. Their hypocrisy made me feel iller than I already was. Poor Karim. What would he do? Get married, join the Baath Party, have lots of kids?

As for joining Rupert in Indonesia, he could forget it. I could scarcely hobble to the loo, let alone get on a plane.

Some friends came to see me shortly afterwards. 'Do you think you'll ever go back?' they asked.

'No, definitely not,' I retorted swiftly. 'It has changed my *entire* perspective on travel. Next time it's Provence for me.'

Six weeks later, however, I found myself on a plane bound for Beirut where, as part of a press trip, I stayed for two days, before driving over the Lebanese mountains back to Damascus. One night I traced my steps through the streets of the old city, surprised that I could still do so, and found my way to Jihad's house.

His door was looking as battered and derelict as ever. It was locked, but when I pushed gently it more or less fell off its rotten hinges. I slid it to one side and stepped into the gloomy room. There was a frantic scrabbling and a black shadow leaped onto the window ledge. It was Beebee. When I called his name he froze and looked at me mistrustfully. He was as scabby as ever. I crossed the room to the bed. Everything looked the same – the girlie pictures on the wall, the dilapidated sofa, the old oil stove, the clothes line over which Jihad had flung his clothes. It felt odd to be standing there again without Jihad. I could not believe that anyone could live in such a place; it looked awful.

I dropped a packet of photographs I had taken over the summer on the bed, together with a couple of trendy T-shirts I had bought in a Soho boutique. They were short, stylishly cut little numbers with a high Lycra content. One was white with black piping around the sleeves, neck and waist. The other was V-necked with cap sleeves and was only navel length. Pity I won't see him in that, I thought. I wrote a brief, simple note and left.

As I was closing the door I heard a noise behind me. A tall old woman with long, frizzy dark grey hair visible beneath a loose headscarf was putting a pail down on the flags. She had dark arched eyebrows, a large hooked nose and high cheekbones. She cut an imposing figure. She was clearly Jihad's mother, whom I had never met before.

'Where is Jihad?' I asked in Arabic.

She looked at me appraisingly. 'Deir es Zor,' she replied. She had a deep, husky voice.

'Why?'

'Work.'

'My name is Robert. I am his friend. I am from England. On the bed there are some photos and a present. They are for him. From me.' I always spoke like this in Arabic, condensing concepts to their most essential elements.

The woman looked at me with her dark eyes. She had a firm straight mouth like a trap. She did not smile, but gestured to the staircase. '*Tofodal*,' she said.

'*Shukran*,' I responded, putting my right hand on my heart as a sign that I was declining her invitation. I was not going to press the hospitality button this time. '*Masa al kheir*,' I added, turning to leave.

'*Masa an-noor*,' she replied, and, picking up the pail, she turned to mount the outdoor staircase in the corner of the courtyard. She was going home and I back to London loneliness. While I could travel all over the world, Jihad was stuck, stateless, in Syria. I would never see him again.

On my last day in Damascus I visited George Dahdah, a very old man who sold antiquities from one of the rooms in his gracious old house. I had been held up and was an hour late for our appointment. He came to the door rather shakily, and when he saw me he held up both his hands and cast his eyes to the heavens. 'I am terribly sorry,' I said.

'I am an old man,' he replied by way of remonstration.

'I'm sorry,' I repeated almost petulantly. We sounded like old lovers. He led me into his charming courtyard. Here and there cats were sunning themselves on the marble tiles. A small fountain plashed into a marble bowl in the middle.

Mr Dahdah sat down. He told me, as old men do, about his life: how he set up the first tourist agency in Syria; how during the Mandate they started charging the French officers ten times what ordinary people were charged to go round the Great Mosque and the Azem Palace (things hadn't changed); how he had had three wives, including an American woman. How he had started dealing in expensive antiques. How in the seventies no one used to come to Syria from the West.

'No one even spoke English. They ripped up all the books, you know. They were stupid. But now they are all learning again in the schools and now everyone wants old Dahdah. All the time I have the television cameras here. Yesterday I was on Dutch TV. Things are changing in Syria now.' He suddenly looked at me shrewdly through the fading irises of his hazel eyes. 'What do you do in Syria?' he asked.

I thought for a second and said, 'I am a writer and journalist and I am going to write a book about your country.'

There, now I had said it, and with the enunciation came all the relief that greeted the man who screamed 'King Midas has got donkeys' ears!' into the sea. There was no more need to lie; I was going home the next day. Not even Jihad had known who I really was. At last, the sheer joy of being myself.

'Ah, my dear,' said Mr Dahdah, 'be very, very clever with what you write. Or else ...' He performed a dismembering motion with his hands. '*They* will tear it all up to pieces. Be very, very careful. They have the power. They can destroy everything.' He gave a high-pitched whistling laugh. 'Now old Dahdah is very tired. He must go to bed. To sleep.'

He shuffled off down the corridor and let me out into the anonymous, secretive old Arab street.